KU-329-731

Gender and Citizenship

The Dialectics of Subject-Citizenship in Nineteenth-Century French Literature and Culture

CLAUDIA MOSCOVICI

ROWMAN & LITTLEFIELD PUBLISHERS, INC.
Lanham • Boulder • New York • Oxford

ROWMAN & LITTLEFIELD PUBLISHERS, INC.

Published in the United States of America
by Rowman & Littlefield Publishers, Inc.
4720 Boston Way, Lanham, Maryland 20706
http://www.rowmanlittlefield.com

12 Hid's Copse Road
Comnor Hill, Oxford OX2 9JJ, England

Copyright © 2000 by Rowman & Littlefield Publishers, Inc.

All rights reserved. No part of this publication may be reproduced,
stored in a retrieval system, or transmitted in any form or by any
means, electronic, mechanical, photocopying, recording, or otherwise,
without the prior permission of the publisher.

British Library Cataloguing in Publication Information Available

Library of Congress Cataloging-in-Publication Data

Moscovici, Claudia, 1969–
    Gender and citizenship : the dialectics of subject-citizenship in nineteenth-
century French literature and culture / Claudia Moscovici.
        p.   cm.
    Includes bibliographical references and index.
    ISBN 0-8476-9694-4 (cloth : alk. paper) — ISBN 0-8476-9695-2 (pbk. : alk. paper)
    1. French literature—19th century—History and criticism.   2. Gender identity
in literature.   3. Androgyny (Psychology) in literature.   I. Title.

PQ283 .M64   2000
840.9'353—dc21   99-087268

Printed in the United States of America

♾™ The paper used in this publication meets the minimum requirements of
American National Standard for Information Sciences—Permanence of
Paper for Printed Library Materials, ANSI/NISO Z39.48-1992.

Contents

Acknowledgments

I would like to express my gratitude to the colleagues and friends who encouraged me during the process of writing this book. Above all, I would like to thank my former dissertation adviser, Nancy Armstrong, for her lucid critiques. I would also like to thank my readers, Ross Chambers and Linda Nicholson, for their insightful commentaries and helpful suggestions. Likewise, I feel indebted to my editor at Rowman & Littlefield, Adrienne Hervé, for her efficiency, patience and support.

A version of the chapter "Gendered Spheres in Balzac's *La Cousine Bette*" appeared in the *International Journal of Politics, Culture and Society* (1997): 469–496.

I am grateful to my colleagues and friends at the College of General Studies of Boston University—including Michael Kort, Michael Mahon, Natalie McKnight, Jim Sheets, Henry Wend, Robert Wexelblatt, and Jim Wilcox—for creating a collegial atmosphere free of scholarly dogma and full of open-minded intellectual support.

Last but not least, I would like to thank my immediate family—my husband, Dan Troyka; my parents, Henri and Elvira Moscovici; and my children, Alex and Sophie Moscovici-Troyka—for their unwavering love and encouragement. Without them and the child-care help of my mother-in-law, Robbie Troyka, and of my friend, Shen Lin Hu, I could not have completed this book.

Introduction: The Dialectics of Subject-Citizenship

Just as the eighteenth century is known for instituting a masculine, republican model of citizenship,[1] so the nineteenth century should be known for producing an ambisexual, "social" model of citizenship[2] that explains women's precarious power today. The phenomenon of androgyny, or the dialectical combination of male and female sexual characteristics, offers a key to understanding this cultural and political transition in models of subject-citizenship. Rousseau is perhaps the best-known eighteenth-century French author to invoke the trope of androgyny to elaborate a masculine model of citizenship. In *Emile, ou de l'éducation* (1762), Rousseau observes, "In everything not related to sex, woman is man: she has the same organs, needs, faculties" (465).[3]

For Rousseau, androgyny implies a masculine identity that provides the standard of humanity. While man has no gender, woman is endowed with two. She combines masculine (or human) faculties with feminine sexual characteristics. Woman and man are identical—"woman is man," that is— except insofar as sexuality is concerned. Man comes to represent human identity by negating the sexual characteristics ascribed to woman. "There is no equality between the sexes when it comes to gender," Rousseau famously observes. "Man is man only at certain times; woman is woman all her life, or at least all her youth" (470). Interestingly, what makes women sexual is not desire, but reproduction—pregnancy and child-birth—precisely the qualities that men lack. In Rousseau's ontology, men's lack represents a gain. Not having the ability to be pregnant, give birth or lactate establishes the boundaries of the truly human. It is the sexual side of human nature, Rousseau further suggests, that poses a threat to his imagined republic. Sexuality leads women to uncontrollable passions and emotions that would overwhelm the asexual, or masculine, equanimity needed to manage the public domain.

Rousseau's social order relies upon an asymmetrical positioning of women in relation to men. Men come into being as democratic citizen-subjects by eliminating the qualities attributed to women. The process of defining the male subject in terms of what he is not—as not being a female—pursues the logic of what I will call, adopting Hegelian terminology, a "single dialectic." The category of Emile as a "rational man" is created by negating irrationality from its definition and projecting that quality upon women. In this semiotic relation, the category "woman" has no identity of its own acquired, in turn, by means of the negation of masculine characteristics. Republican discourse therefore utilizes a single dialectical process to depict women as nonsubjects.

Just as the new citizen-subject must negate supposedly feminine qualities, so the new masculine republic must be free of women. Emile's entrance into the social world depends upon contact with other boys. Homosocial bonds condition young men to respect the equality of fellow citizens. In Rousseau's imagined republic, "Independence and equality would endow my acquaintanceships with all the candor of goodwill" (456). Only after integrating into a homosocial environment—the necessary step for entering the public sphere—can Emile begin to think about reproducing that order with a female mate. If we pursue the logic of the single dialectic, however, we observe that the superiority of the male public sphere could not be established without some standard of comparison.

The newly created private sphere provides the necessary contrast. Sophie, or the "ideal" mate for Emile, comes into the scene in the fifth and last section of the text, with the understanding that "Marriage will make [Emile] a full member of the community." Rousseau could not make woman's secondary status—as well as her necessity to the production of masculine citizenship—more clear than when he states: "After having tried to form natural man, to complete our work, let us see how the woman who agrees with this man should be fashioned" (473).

Does this single dialectical definition of the citizen-subject relegate woman to the status of beast? Not in Rousseau's sexual ontology. Woman cannot be represented as an animal if she is to prove a good helpmate for man in the new democratic society. To fulfill her feminine duties—and, more important, to enable man to be a good citizen—woman, too, must be educated and rational. Once he describes woman as rational, however, Rousseau encounters a potential problem. Having defined reason as inherently masculine—that is, as the absence of feminine characteristics—how can he "androgynously" attribute some rationality to woman?

Rousseau examines this problem at length. He asks, "Are women capable of serious reasoning? is it important that they cultivate it? . . . is its cultivation useful to the functions they must perform?" (501). Ultimately, the author compromises his single dialectical model of citizenship. He proposes a more nuanced conception of reason, distinguishing between masculine and feminine types of reasoning. "The obedience and faithfulness that she owes her husband, the tenderness and care that she owes her children, are such natural and sensible consequences of her condition that she cannot . . . refuse to follow the internal feeling that guides her" (501). To be androgynous, woman's reason must remain connected to her sexual nature and, more specifically, to the reproductive characteristics that men lack. Once masculine reasoning is defined dialectically as the lack of feminine reasoning, the republican model of citizenship is momentarily preserved.

Rousseau's goal of reaching a purely masculine citizen-subject by means of a dialectical process of negation of feminine characteristics, however, is doomed to failure. In fact, reading cultural identity in terms of the dialectic leads us to acknowledge the fundamental androgyny of subjects. When one subject requires the exclusion of qualities associated with another subject to create his identity, those excluded qualities become part and parcel of the first subject's self-definition. In depending upon the negation of feminine qualities, it stands to reason that the category of "man" simultaneously incorporates the concept of "nonman" or "woman." Insofar as it depends upon a dialectical articulation, the subject is inherently androgynous.

So far, however, we have only examined one kind of androgyny, achieved by means of a single dialectical process, whereby two beings, one male and one female, are positioned in hierarchical and oppositional relations. While this paradigm of identity may describe the republican model of citizenship, it does not adequately describe the more reciprocal relationships between men and women that developed during the nineteenth century. As much as *Emile* uses the figure of androgyny to construct citizenship as masculine, nineteenth-century authors will reformulate this trope to disturb the neat hierarchy between men and women. As the writings of Sand, Balzac, and Comte (among others) illustrate, less than one hundred years after the publication of *Emile*, it is precisely Sophie's qualities—her sympathetic and nurturing nature—that help create an ambisexual model of subject-citizenship.

My book will trace the conceptual and cultural transformation from a masculine to an androgynous model of citizenship in terms of the dialectic. Nineteenth-century readings of androgyny are symptomatic of the emergence of what I call, borrowing Luce Irigaray's terms, a "chiasmic" or "double dialectical" model of gender relations that gives women a civic power that eighteenth-century texts deliberately withheld. This model of gender increasingly predominates over the single dialectical or republican model of gender introduced by Rousseau and systematized by Hegel.

By using a dialectical model of androgyny to interpret shifts in models of citizenship, my book revises two kinds of twentieth-century readings of gender roles in nineteenth-century (mainly) French literary and philosophical texts: (1) those that represent femininity only as the negative of masculinity (as nonmasculinity) and argue that women are relegated to the private sphere and virtually deprived of subject-citizenship status, and (2) those that attempt to correct gender asymmetries by idealizing nineteenth-century literary representations of androgyny, where androgyny is understood as a union of the sexes.

I illustrate that both kinds of contemporary interpretations read nineteenth-century French culture according to the logic of the Hegelian single dialectic. Feminist (or even nonfeminist) readings of gender that define femininity simply as nonmasculinity ignore the important power exercised by women in their roles as mothers, wives, educators, and regulators of social policies during the nineteenth century. Notably, Carolyn Heilbrun's *Toward a Recognition of Androgyny*[4] analyzes literary and philosophical representations of androgyny in Western culture to show that androgyny can eliminate gender distinctions and the accompanying sexual hierarchies. Despite this objective, she defines androgyny in terms of the single dialectic, as the union of a male subject and a nonmale subject (or his female negation). This definition of androgyny, which represents gender only in terms of a male subject and its series of negations and fusions, can only remain androcentric and ignore the role of women in culture and society. The problem with twentieth-century interpretations of nineteenth-century gender roles derives from the unacknowledged historical continuity between the two. Both models, indeed, most theories of the modern sex/gender system, are indebted to a particularly androcentric type of theory of gendering, the Hegelian single dialectic, where the female subject is viewed only as a nonmale subject rather than being acknowledged as having her own civic identity.

To correct how we read our nineteenth-century predecessors in a way that accounts for women's participation in citizenship, I propose to examine gender in terms of a "double dialectical" relation between the sexes. In the single dialectic of gender, women are described as the negation of the male positive term, such that the dialectical process begins and ends with an emphasis on maleness. By contrast, the double dialectic understands men and women to be both positive and negative terms—each defined as not the other—leading to a model of citizenship that accounts for women's civic power.

In addition to emphasizing (potential) sexual parity, the double dialectic depicts a process of sexual mixture, or androgyny, that poses a challenge to models of sexual purity proposed by writers such as Rousseau. As noted, the dialectic depicts the process whereby two subjects that are regarded as opposites simultaneously negate and incorporate the qualities associated with their counterparts. If we assume men and women to be inherently androgynous, however, are we led to the conclusion that we have reached a postmodern era beyond sexual identity? No. On the contrary, the dialectical process of forming an androgynous identity illustrates that even a fusion of two beings does not eliminate their differences, as an erroneous understanding of the dialectic as a process of thesis-antithesis-synthesis would suggest. Sexual categories are not erased, but undergo sublation or a process of selective incorporation and negation of both masculine and female traits into two new androgynous beings. Consequently, by incorporating and negating select qualities of male and female subjects, the androgyne simultaneously preserves and cancels the difference between them.

Using androgyny as a method of describing the double dialectical relations between the sexes, I read the different versions of gendered citizenship elaborated by Georg Wilhelm Friedrich Hegel's *Phenomenology of Spirit* (1807) and *Philosophy of Right* (1821), George Sand's *Indiana* (1832), Honoré de Balzac's *La Cousine Bette* (1846), Auguste Comte's *Une Esquisse Générale du Positivisme* (1851–1854), and the journal of the hermaphrodite Herculine Barbin (1860). Comte's and Balzac's models of citizenship observe a double dialectics of gender because they take both masculine and feminine subjects as points of departure for their definitions of subject-citizenship. That is to say, they define the masculine subject by the exclusion of feminine qualities and the feminine subject, in turn, by the exclusion of masculine qualities.

Like Hegel, Comte achieves a division of spheres by rhetorically manipulating not only gender stereotypes, but also the political categories of the times, particularly the distinction between duties and rights. He defines women primarily in terms of the interpersonal social duties facilitated by their "sympathetic" natures. Then he sets masculinity in opposition to the duties assigned to women and, in this way, arrogates to men certain abstract individual rights. What begins as a division of labor between masculine rights and feminine duties by virtue of the first two moves of Comtean dialectics will finally undergo sublation.

Comte uses the notion of women's familial and social duties to argue for their rights, including their right to public education equivalent to that of men. At the same time, by making feminine duty function as a means of civilizing what he regards as "selfish" rights-based masculine versions of citizenship, he feminizes the Hegelian model of citizenship. Still divided along gender lines, the ideal citizen also overcomes those divisions to incorporate both feminine sympathies and masculine force and practicality. In other words, Comte's model of citizenship is androgynous. While this double dialectics of gender may help empower women in some social functions, it nonetheless continues to exclude them from political self-representation.

The mechanisms of the double dialectical model of citizenship, including its simultaneous improvement and restriction of women's social conditions, become more evident in Balzac's *La Cousine Bette*. Much like Comte's text, Balzac's novel attempts to strengthen women's social roles while also weakening their political power. The novelist, too, observes a dialectical process of gendering ridden with internal contradictions. Balzac's novel begins by centralizing the social role of Mme Hulot, the ideal mother–wife. M. Hulot, the bourgeois husband, is described as the cultural opposite or negation of his wife. If Mme Hulot, the figure of the mother–wife, is virtuous, self-restrained, and chaste, then, according to the pattern we can observe in Comte and throughout so many central documents of nineteenth-century culture, M. Hulot, the figure of the father–husband, will have to embody anything but those qualities. In the first loop of the dialectical process by which the novel produces gender differences, M. Hulot's existence, and, by extension, the social identity of the father–husband, is articulated primarily in terms of his contradictory relations to his wife, who becomes the model citizen.

To follow the second loop of the double dialectics, Balzac's narrative begins with M. Hulot, the masculine subject, whom he depicts in terms of his political participation in the public sphere. Hulot was a baron, a protégé and a high officer in Napoleon's army, and later a director of the Ministry of War in Louis-Philippe's July Monarchy. We are also told that Mme Hulot had (at least early in their marriage) every reason to revere him and to wish for an identity as the wife of Baron Hulot. Thus, in the second loop of the double dialectics, the husband is defined in what could be called a "positive" way: he is not simply the negation of "woman." Indeed, the feminine subject has become secondary to and is defined in terms of the masculine subject, exactly inverting the earlier relationship of masculine to feminine.

Balzac's narrative, however, poses an obstacle to the fulfillment of this logic of gender formation. The novel raises the following questions: What happens when the difference between men and women fails to keep women from becoming involved in the masculine public sphere? What happens, more specifically, when economic circumstances force women to become part of the working force and thereby accumulate influence in the public sphere? This problem emerges as Cousine Bette represents animal aggression in a female body. Propelled by economic circumstances, the androgynous woman, defined as the selective incorporation and partial negation of both male and female identities, disrupts the system of difference that Balzac attempts to establish.

Sand's *Indiana* is understandably more self-conscious of the problems inherent in the division of spheres than either Comte's or Balzac's works. Published in 1832, this novel obviously predates Comte's and Balzac's texts. Nonetheless, Sand's critical representation of gender places her, at least ideologically, closer to twentieth-century critiques of gender roles than to the nineteenth-century division of spheres. To launch a critique to this effect, she creates nonconformist characters who subvert the social categories her successors would strive to keep in place. What makes Indiana capable of disturbing a fundamentally binary system, I will argue, is the fact that she overcomes or sublates both the male and female identities of her fictional context. She embodies the full double dialectic.

For Sand, the female protagonist does not negate whatever qualities her culture associates with the male protagonist. Although it may be true that Sand establishes a set of oppositions between her heroine's qualities and those of the male protagonists—by contrasting, for example, Indiana's delicacy with her husband's indelicacy, her virtue with her lover's lack of virtue—this novel makes it all too obvious that the male characters do not operate as the desirable norm in relation to which the woman is found lacking. On the contrary, more often than not, it is the very conventional quality of Sand's male characters that validates, by contrast, the heroine's claims to ideal fulfillment of the category of human. Equally important, Indiana's exemplary violation of gender norms is closely linked to her struggle against other forms of domination, including slavery. By means of Indiana's idealized androgyny, I argue, Sand's aesthetics become intimately linked to the politics of utopia.

Unlike nineteenth-century French fiction, the latest contemporary criticism cautions against idealizing androgyny. Most notably, in his introduction to the diary of a nineteenth-century hermaphrodite named Herculine Barbin, Foucault attempts to resist the temptation of describing androgyny as a utopian construct. Foucault's analysis of Herculine's diary accomplishes three main goals: (1) it undermines positivist readings of the body; (2) it explains the process by which sexual identity becomes a substitute for civic identity during the nineteenth century; and (3) it argues that androgyny can offer a freer mode of defining identity than binary formulations of gender.

In my own analysis of Herculine's diary, while acknowledging Foucault's important contributions to the study of the relations between sexuality and citizenship, I illustrate the hidden complicity between positivist and Foucauldian readings of gender in their definition of the subject as implicitly masculine and of femininity as the negation of masculinity. In the chapter devoted to Herculine's story, I use the hermaphrodite's rather pessimistic account of her experiences both as a woman and as a man to question Foucault's historical distinction between her early experience of an indeterminate sexuality in a feminine milieu and one where she is confined by biology in the masculine public sphere. I argue that Foucault constitutes this binary relationship between a masculinized modern world and a feminized nonmodern world because his model of gender relations is (at least initially) motivated by the logic of the single dialectic.

Throughout my book, I argue that both patterns of gender formation—the single and double dialectics—lead us to acknowledge the fundamental androgyny of the citizen-subject. I show how the binary organization of sexual difference depends upon the relational combinations of the historically defined terms *man* and *woman,* which are never pure even at their very beginning. When sex is treated as a natural and unchangeable characteristic with which we are born, men and women are viewed as separate and unmixed sexual identities. It is clear to everyone that men are not women and women are not men. The concept of androgyny allows me to demonstrate not only that men and women share some common human features, but also (and more pertinent for current feminist criticism) that the process of gender formation already assumes that sexual identity is a mixture.

Looking at subject-citizenship in terms of two kinds of androgynies—one that follows a single dialectical or androcentric pattern and the second that follows a double dialectical or ambisexual pattern—allows us to perceive the difference between and the historical transition from relational definitions of gender that are asymmetrical (and tend to privilege male subjects) to those that are symmetrical (and tend to accommodate both male and female subjects on equivalent terms). The single dialectical pattern is androgynous in the sense that the category of women is intrinsic to definitions of men. In this first pattern of androgyny, women do not have a cultural identity of their own that is formed by means of the negation of the category of men. In the double dialectical pattern of androgyny, both men and women are taken as points of departure for definitions of subjectivity since each sex is defined as the negation of the other sex. It is only this double dialectical pattern of androgyny that endows women with a cultural identity that secures their paradoxical roles[5] as both representatives of and outsiders to subject-citizenship in nineteenth-century French society.

NOTES

1. See Carole Pateman's explanation of the republican model of citizenship in *The Sexual Contract*.

2. See Denise Riley's historical analysis of the emergence of the social model of citizenship in *Am I That Name: Feminism and the Category of "Women" in History*.

3. All short passages, including citations from *Emile, ou de l'éducation* (Paris: Flammarion, 1966), are my own translations. I use standard translations for the texts that I cite at length, including the narratives of Hegel, Comte, Balzac, Sand, and Herculine Barbin.

4. See Carolyn Heilbrun's *Toward a Recognition of Androgyny*.

5. In *Only Paradoxes to Offer*, Scott observes that the history of women's participation in citizenship functions is fraught with paradoxes and contradictions. She states, "The history of feminism can be understood as an interplay between a repetitious pattern of exclusion and a changing articulation of subjects. . . . But the terms of exclusion are also variable and contradictory, based in different epistemologies, and this variability and contradiction result in fundamentally different conceptions of the 'women' whose rights are being claimed" (14).

1

Theoretical Foundations: Doubling the Dialectic

Why employ a Hegelian concept, namely, the dialectic, to account for the transitions in models of French citizenship? I believe that Hegel's elaboration of the dialectic explains better than any other conceptual framework how the notion of the modern citizen comes into being in a discourse that draws explicit connections among gender, subjectivity, knowledge, and power.[1] The *Phenomenology of Spirit*[2] narrates the story of the formation of the subject. Hegel posits that reality (or "absolute" truth) must not be thought of only as "Substance," under the form of either a thinking consciousness or a nonthinking object. Reality incorporates both the knowing subject and the known object. The philosopher calls "Ego," "Substance," or "Subject" this combination of agency and process of knowledge. In sections 18–20 of the Preface, he explains:

> Further, the living Substance is being which is in truth Subject, or, what is the same, is in truth actual only in so far as it is the movement of positing itself, or is the mediation of its self-othering within itself. This Substance is, as Subject, pure, *simple negativity*, and is for this very reason the bifurcation of the simple; it is the doubling which sets up opposition, and then again the negation of this indifferent diversity and of its antithesis [the immediate simplicity]. Only this self-*restoring* sameness, or this reflection in otherness within itself—not an *original* or *immediate* unity as such—is the True. It is the process of its own becoming, the circle that presupposes its end as its goal, having its end also as its beginning; and only by being worked out to its end, is it actual. (*Phenomenology of Spirit*, 10)

The Ego, according to Hegel, does not embody a personified thinker.[3] It is a logical operation that eliminates internal contradictions to offer access to objective and noncontradictory knowledge of "the True" or "the Whole."[4] Likewise, the subject's knowledge is not "an original or immediate unity." The quest for truth requires a difficult dialectical evolution. This process repeatedly projects "doubling which sets up opposition," only to negate these contradictions and attain "self-restoring sameness." The Hegelian dialectic represents a conceptual and historical process[5] that achieves progress by means of a series of sublations, or negations of undesirable qualities and incorporation of desirable ones into a later stage of development. Without systematic labor, Hegel cautions, knowledge sinks "into mere edification, and even insipidity, . . . it lacks the seriousness, the suffering, the patience, and the labor of the negative" (10). Hegel proceeds to detail the dialectical moves of the subject as well as to explain their purpose. In the famous section "Self-Consciousness, Lordship and Bondage," he offers an allegorical description of formation of the subject.

Hegel perceives the human being as dual. We are composed of a body that makes us dependent upon nature and a mind that can elevate us to the level of pure thought. Hegel attempts to solve the following problem: How can human beings free themselves of their lower, physical nature and attain their higher destiny as pure thought? To purify the body of its natural characteristics, Hegel engages mind and body in a dialectical relationship. He personifies the mind as "the master" and the body as "the slave."[6] The relationship between master and slave must enable both sides of our beings—body and mind—to achieve a purer state of being. In his relationship to the master, the slave becomes a thinking subject by working for the master (since work, argues Hegel, implies thought) and by fearing for his life in his life-and-death struggle with the master. The slave's fear of annihilation makes him see his life go before his eyes, thereby negating the lower physical existence that had defined his being.

Likewise, the master is also improved by the dialectical process. The relationship to the slave allows the master to gain recognition as a thinking subject. Hegel explains: "Self-consciousness exists in and for itself when, and by the fact that, it so exists for another; that it exists only in being acknowledged. . . . The detailed exposition of the Notion of spiritual unity in its duplication will present us with the process of Recognition" (111). According to Hegel, subjectivity is formed only in and by a social world. Rather than being solitary, the self acquires identity through recognition by other subjects.[7]

To come into existence, the initial and primary "Ego" (let us say, subject A) projects another contrary subject or "Alter Ego" (subject non-A).[8] It is interesting to see how and why Hegel attempts to persuade us that the self develops not only intersubjectively, but also by means of a process of negation. In the sections entitled "Consciousness" and "Force and Understanding," Hegel explains:

> In the play of Forces this law showed itself to be precisely this absolute transition and pure change; the self-same viz Force splits into an antithesis which at first appears to be an independent difference, but which in fact proves to be none; for it is the self-same which repels itself from itself, and therefore what is repelled is essentially self-attractive, for it is the same; the difference created since it is no difference . . . is nothing else but the selfsame that has repelled itself from itself, and therefore merely posits an antithesis which is none. (96)

In this first step of the single dialectic, Hegel begins with "subject A" and argues that the subject gains a sense of self only by distinguishing himself from other subjects and objects. Consequently, Hegel defines identity negatively. He only articulates what the subject is not. Defining identity in this fashion fulfills three functions. First, it elaborates the semantic process whereby the identity of each concept is established by a process of differentiation from other concepts, a setting off from what that concept is not. This axiom has been adopted by Saussurian linguistics and, though much contested by other kinds of linguistic theories, has proven helpful to structuralist and poststructuralist scholarship.

Second, negation constitutes the central mechanism of Hegel's dialectical system. Following an initial negation, the single dialectical process continues by synthesizing the initial contraries, subject A and subject non-A, into a new subject, subject non-non-A. The double negation eliminates some of the undesirable qualities of the first two subjects while preserving some of their desirable characteristics. As Hegel explains, "*Supercession* exhibits its true twofold meaning which we have seen in the negative: it is at once a *negating* and a *preserving*" (68). Hegel calls this third movement of the dialectic the "negative of the negative," since it results from the negation of subject A, followed by the synthesis and negation of subject A and its opposite, subject non-A. The new subject, or subject non-non-A, in turn projects a negative and the single dialectical process continues until all contradictions and physical characteristics are eliminated from the initial subject A.

This explanation leads us to the third, sociopolitical, implication of the Hegelian dialectic. Because Hegel describes difference as a projection of the "selfsame," he ultimately assimilates difference into sameness.[9] The philosopher indicates that the second subject is not really different from the first subject—"the difference created . . . is no difference . . . is nothing else but the selfsame"—since this subject only exists as a semiotic field excluded from the identity of the first subject, subject A. In other words, the second subject is only a negative projection of the "selfsame," the first subject. As we have observed with respect to non-A's relationship to A, all of the dialectically derived subjects continue to be defined in terms of the original subject A. Consequently, they have no identity of their own. Instead, these derivative subjects help establish and purify the identity of the "selfsame."

What concerns us at this point about Hegel's dialectical system is that it begins with a single subject that is (only apparently) internally divided and ends with a single subject that is unified. The categories of difference and division (that will become important to subsequent postmodernist and psychoanalytic definitions of the "split subject") function only as the means by which a single subject eventually achieves coherence and totality. This instrumentalization of the notion of difference by means of a single dialectical formation of subjectivity plays an important role in Hegel's conception of masculine citizenship, as elaborated both in the *Phenomenology of Spirit* and in the *Philosophy of Right*. These texts relegate the feminine subject to the status of nonsubject by means of a dialectical process that begins and ends with a masculine subject.

In the *Philosophy of Right*, Hegel describes the ethical and civic relations between husband and wife in much the same way he described the more abstract relations between the ego (or master) and alter-ego (or slave) in the *Phenomenology of Spirit*. He regards the family as the product of a supercession of opposites, in which "The difference of the sexes and their ethical content remains, however, in the unity of the substance, and its movement is just the constant becoming of that substance" (*Philosophy of Right*, 276). According to Hegelian logic, the husband represents the norm or the ego, the wife his negation or alter ego, and the nuclear family is the sublation of these two ethical contraries. Hegel argues that, following the synthesis of masculine and feminine roles, "the difference of the sexes and their ethical content remains" (276). The figures of man and woman continue, nonetheless, their dialectical development: "The husband is sent out by the Spirit of the Family into the community in which he finds his self-conscious being" (276). His ethics are primarily governed by human law. The wife, on the other hand, remains enclosed within the domestic sphere. She is in charge of the "natural" ties of family and of the "universal" duties of burying and honoring the dead, as required by divine law.[10]

Hegel maintains that he is not establishing a hierarchy between the roles of men and women—"Neither of the two is by itself absolutely valid; human law proceeds in its living process from the divine, the law valid on earth from that of the nether world, the conscious from the unconscious" (276)—when, in fact, this is precisely what he is doing. If we accept his premise that subjectivity is active, is rational, and functions primarily in a civic sphere, then we see how woman, who is described in terms of qualities excluded from rationality (she is intuitive, "immediate," and "unconscious"), represents the nonsubject who helps establish the subjectivity of man.[11] The identity of the male subject is consolidated in "the community in which he finds his self-conscious being." By contrast, woman's role is determined by the less-defined "universal" laws of nature that demand respect for the dead and the "natural" affective ties that preserve the nuclear family. By means of a dialectical process that defines the male citizen, Hegel marginalizes woman from active citizenship while at the same time making her central to the construction of the male citizen.

The husband is clearly the principal subject in the family since, as Hegel insists, the family exists to develop man's civic and political identity. To find his self-conscious being, the husband must pass through a series of dialectical oppositions that allow him, as the embodiment of Spirit (*Geist*), to resolve his internal contradictions. In the family, those contradictions are projected upon an external(ized) being, defined as the wife. Without stating that he values man above woman, Hegel shows that the role of woman is instrumental to the formation of a self-conscious masculine subject who, "through consciousness . . . becomes existence and activity" in a social world. Woman is prevented by definition from active participation in the civic sphere. By extension, she remains unacknowledged as a citizen-subject in the community. Being deprived of subject-citizenship in the civic sphere, woman is also deprived of it in the family.

Hegel elaborates, "The family, as person, has its real external existence in property; and it is only when this property takes the form of capital that it becomes the embodiment of the substantial personality of the family" (116). The philosopher describes the family as a form of alliance where the possession and distribution of capital among its members count more than affective bonds. Hegel's alliance-based model of the family obviously predates the formation of the modern nuclear family, the kind of family depicted, for instance, by Sand, Balzac, and Comte. Since married women cannot inherit or own property, then, Hegel deduces, "The family as a legal entity in relation to others must be represented by the husband as its head. Further, it is his prerogative to go out and work for its living, to attend to its needs, and to control and administer its capital" (116). The civic identity of the male citizen-subject is implicitly determined by the functions from which women are excluded: owning property, working in the public sphere, administering family capital. What is left for woman to do in this semantic and political economy? Hegel prescribes the status of women in his discussion of duties and rights:

> Duty is primarily a relation to something which from my point of view is substantive, absolutely universal. A right, on the other hand, is simply the embodiment of this substance and thus is the particular aspect of it and enshrines my particular freedom. Hence at abstract levels, right and duty appear parcelled out on different sides or in different persons. (*Philosophy of Right*, 12)

Hegel sets up a division of labor between men and women by means of a dialectical definition of duty versus right. Masculine identity is established by rights that "enshrine [one's] particular freedom." These rights are made possible, in turn, by the exclusion of duties that are relegated to the feminine subject.

The distinction between feminine duties and masculine rights, however, only accounts for the first step of the dialectic, which outlines the division of labor within the family. The second step, which deals with the masculine civic sphere and the state, synthesizes (formerly) feminine duties and (formerly) masculine rights to produce a universal masculine subject:

> In the state, as something ethical, as the inter-penetration of the substantive and the particular, my obligation to what is substantive is at the same time the embodiment of my particular freedom. This means that in the state duty and right are united in one and the same relation. (12)

Hegel depicts the masculine subject as engaged in a contractual relationship to other such subjects in the civic sphere and to the laws that govern social interactions in the state. Following this supercession, the masculine subject whose identity emerged by negating feminine duties in the family becomes an improved, more complete subject that combines both feminine duties and masculine rights in the civic sphere. This new masculine subject thus incorporates and transforms feminine duty into a masculine, and hence purer and more self-aware, role that balances obligations to other citizens with individual rights as a citizen in the modern nation-state.

The third step of the dialectic further consolidates the identity of the masculine citizen-subject. Hegel proceeds to redistribute duty and right along class, not only gender, lines. He qualifies that duties and rights constitute the two facets of the same dialectical process only for a class of propertied free men:

> The absolute identity of right and duty in the state is present in these spheres not as a genuine identity but only as a similarity of content, because in them this content is determined as quite general and is simply the fundamental

principle of both right and duty, i.e., the principle that men, as persons, are free. (161)

The philosopher continues to explain that certain classes of men cannot be counted as citizen-subjects because they have not sublated the feminized notion of duty with the masculinized notion of right: "Slaves, therefore, have no duties because they have no rights, and vice versa" (161). The male citizen-subject embodies a concrete universal. He is a universal subject in his collective duties, but a concrete subject in his individual rights. This new civic identity can only emerge from a dialectical process:

> In the course of the inward development of the concrete Idea, however, its moments become distinguished and their specific determinacy becomes at the same time a difference of content. . . . This concept of the union of duty and right is a point of vital importance and in it the inner strength of the state is contained. (161)

According to Hegel, the identity of the citizen-subjects who are the bearers of both duties and rights develops in three stages. The first stage performs a division of spheres between men and women that excludes women from citizenship to create male civic identity. A second stage, while negating femininity, also incorporates feminine duties into masculine rights to produce a more complete masculine subject. Finally, the third stage divides that masculine subject into different classes of men, some of whom have duties and rights, others of whom have "no duties because they have no rights and vice versa." It is only through a double negation, or differentiation from both women and other classes of men, that propertied men acquire their modern identities as citizens who embody the "union of duty and right . . . [in which] the inner strength of the state is contained."

Hegel's formulation of masculine citizenship has been so influential for nineteenth-century social and political theory that contemporary feminist critics could not afford to ignore it. As Naomi Schor puts it quite bluntly: "There is no understanding women's exile from civil society without rereading Hegel."[12] Luce Irigaray has been one of the few feminist philosophers to investigate the cultural and political effects of the Hegelian theory of subject-citizenship—namely, how it excludes women from the civic sphere and renders them second-class subjects—and to explain how those effects are inextricably related to a single dialectical process. Irigaray argues that civic parity or equivalence between men and women can only be achieved once both men and women are acknowledged as sexual subjects. If Hegel's single dialectical process yields a unisexual, and in this case masculine, citizen-subject, then, Irigaray reasons, an ambisexual no-

tion of citizenship that includes both men and women would have to follow a double dialectical logic. Thus, Irigaray's critique of Hegel can be
read as an attempt to transform the Hegelian single dialectic of gender
into a double dialectical relationship that supersedes the qualities of both
male and female subjects.

In *Speculum: de l'autre femme*,[13] Irigaray uses the Hegelian dialectic to
address the following question: Even if the self has been historically defined as "masculine," could a feminine subject coexist with the masculine
subject, without, that is, destroying the very distinction between masculinity and femininity on which the definition of the citizen now depends?
In other words, could there be a definition of femininity that does not arise
from a semiotic field excluded from definitions of masculinity? She asks
us to imagine that woman is defined not only as the negation of a masculine subject, but also positively: "Imagine that woman imagines, the
object would lose its character as *idée fixe*" (165). If woman had her own
cultural and semiotic identity, then, Irigaray asks, "[W]hat foundation
would endure for the existence of the 'subject'?" (165). She suggests that
transforming a single dialectic of gender, one that begins with and revolves around a masculine subject, into a double dialectics of gender formation that explains the interactions between two gendered subjects
would transform that phallocentric economy into an ambisexual one capable of including women positively defined.

In mobilizing a Hegelian dialectical framework, Irigaray must consequently double it. According to Irigaray, the process of transformation
begins with the "recognition" of "the negative." In an economy of gender, the "negative" would signify the limits of sexual identity. Establishing such boundaries depends upon an understanding that sexual difference cannot be reduced simply to a negation of the self.[14] "This negative,"
Irigaray maintains, "Hegel never knew it." She explains,

> His negative remains the mastery of conscience, which is historically mas-
> culine, over nature and the human species. The negative of sexual difference
> is the acceptance of the limits of my gender and the recognition of the irre-
> ducibility of the other. It is insurmountable but it gives positive access, nei-
> ther instinctive nor sensory, to the other. (*J'aime à toi*, 32–33)

Irigaray posits that if both masculine and feminine subjects assumed
they were different from each other, a genuine "recognition" between the
sexes could occur:

> It seems to me that the operation that Hegel called Recognition is a means
> of placing in contact, one across from the other, one next to the other, . . . man
> and woman. Recognition is the gesture that could enable us to overcome the

hierarchical domination between the sexes, which could endow woman and man, women and men, with dignity and identity. (*J'aime à toi,* 158)

For Hegel, the mutual recognition between the ego and its projected alter ego constitutes only a brief moment in the dialectic that propels the ego toward self-consciousness. While rejecting both the masculine and the teleological nature of the Hegelian dialectic, Irigaray focuses upon a brief textual moment in Hegel's *Phenomenology* where the self does not view the other as a projection of itself. In this passage, the ego recognizes the alter ego's alterity and is recognized as different by the alter ego in turn:

> Now, this movement of self-consciousness in relation to another self-consciousness has in this way been represented as the action of one self-consciousness, but this action of the one has itself the double significance of being both its own action and the action of the other as well. For the other is equally independent and self-contained, and there is nothing in it of which it is not itself the origin. (*Phenomenology,* 111–112)

The moment of mutual recognition between (what temporarily becomes) two subjects establishes the simultaneously interdependent and separate identities of ego and alter ego. While each subject comes into being by differentiating itself from his counterpart, in this instance, one subject does not treat the other self as an object:

> The first does not have the object before it merely as it exists primarily for desire, but as something that has an independent existence of its own, which, therefore, it cannot utilize for its own purposes, if that object does not of its own accord do what the first does to it. Thus the movement is simply the double movement of two self-consciousnesses. Each sees the other do the same as it does; each does itself what it demands of the other, and therefore also does what it does only in so far as the other does the same. (*Phenomenology,* 112)

The point of juncture where the (arguably) masculine subject recognizes that "it is not everything" constitutes the beginning of a doubling process or, to use Hegel's expression, "the double movement of two self-consciousnesses." To pursue this fold in Hegelian logic would be to understand gender, along with Irigaray, as "a double pole of attraction and support"—meaning a cultural and semantic exchange between feminine and masculine subjects—"which excludes disintegration and rejection, attraction and decomposition" by offering the feminine a relatively independent cultural identity and difference from the masculine (*An Ethics of Sexual Difference,* 19). Such polarity ensures that a principle of difference will articulate "every encounter, promises, alliances" between masculine and feminine subjects (19).

To explain how gender distinctions occur within a fully doubled dialectic, Irigaray invokes the figure of a "chiasmus or a double loop in which each [sex] can go toward the other and come back to itself" (19). The figure of "the chiasmus" refers to "any structure in which elements are repeated in reverse, so giving the pattern ABBA."[15] Relying upon Saussurean premises, we assume that in any language system there are no absolutely positive terms since any sign acquires its meaning *diacritically,* or in a negative relation to other signs. Thus, the word *man* acquires meaning when contrasted to other words that resemble it either phonetically and graphically (such as *tan* or *van*) or conceptually (as in the case of *woman*). Although a diacritical system of language acknowledges no absolute positive terms, we can describe, nonetheless, as "positive" the concepts that serve as the starting points of semantic negation. In a phallocentric world, Irigaray argues, only the term *man* constitutes such a positive term (A), as it acquires meaning by negating the term *woman,* consequently defined as nonman or non-A. Woman drops out of the definitional picture at this point.

By contrast, Irigaray proposes a symbolic economy based on the polarities of the term "A" (or masculinity) and term "B" (or femininity), where A and B continue to be defined by their dialectical interaction. Thus, the point of departure of the chiasmus is two sexed subjects, the starting points of two different sexual economies, that exist in a historically specific double dialectical relationship. In a political economy generated by a "double dialectic," men and women still acquire their identities in opposition or complementarity to one another. They do so, however, by means of a logic that integrates both sexes into a civic sphere where they may debate "the public good." This is precisely the semiotic and cultural process that emerges from my reading of nineteenth-century literature and philosophy.

NOTES

1. In my appropriation of selected aspects of Hegelian philosophy, I emphasize the epistemological dimension of Hegel's thought, more specifically the manner in which his theory of the perfectibility of the subject (or his ontology) is subordinated to, or at least dependent upon, the objective of providing certain knowledge of the world. Hegelian scholarship, however, disagrees concerning whether or not this is the most important dimension of Hegelian philosophy. Some critics treat Hegel's epistemology as the primary axis of his thought. For an example of such criticism, see Tom Rockmore's *On Hegel's Epistemology and*

Contemporary Philosophy and *Hegel's Circular Epistemology*. By way of contrast, the Marxist Hegelian Georg Lukacs reads Hegelian philosophy as an elaboration of an ontology in *Toward the Ontology of Being*. Though most readers of Hegel concede that epistemology and ontology are intertwined in his philosophy, their emphasis on one or the other affects their interpretations of Hegelian thought.

2. I am using J. N. Findlay's translation.

3. As J. N. Findlay states in his foreword to Hegel's *Phenomenology of Spirit,* "The subject of Ego is thus for Hegel not what we ordinarily understand by a personal thinker, but the logical function of universality in a peculiar sort of detachment from its species and instances" (xi).

4. Philosophers widely disagree about whether or not Hegel's dialectical system aims at the eventual resolution of its historical contradictions. Most traditional interpretations have posited the teleological nature of Hegelian philosophy, as I do in my argument. The following interpretation of Hegel's thought, advanced by J. N. Findlay in his foreword to the *Phenomenology,* is typical: "Hegel, however, assumes that this progress must have a final term, a state where knowledge need no longer transcend or correct itself, where it will discover itself in its object and its object in itself, where concept will correspond to object and object to consciousness" (xiv). Two of the most influential readings of the Hegelian dialectic as teleological have been provided by the Marxist critics Alexandre Kojève in *Introduction à la lecture de Hegel* and Herbert Marcuse in *Reason and Revolution: Hegel and the Rise of Social Theory*. Along with Irigaray, I situate my own reading in the more traditional, teleological interpretations of Hegelian philosophy. By way of contrast, one of the most influential and creative interpretations of the Hegelian dialectic as nonteleological is advanced by Slavoj Zizek in *The Sublime Object of Ideology*. Zizek's thesis is that "far from being a story of progressive overcoming, dialectics is for Hegel a systematic notation of the failure of all such attempts—'absolute knowledge' denotes a subjective position which finally accepts 'contradiction' as an internal condition of every identity" (6). My own position, which will become more clear as the argument proceeds, is that there are textual moments—especially in the elaboration of the notion of "recognition"—where Hegel's philosophy undermines what I consider to be its fundamentally teleological project.

5. For an excellent and succinct introduction to Hegel's historicism, see Frederick C. Beiser's "Hegel's Historicism," in *The Cambridge Companion to Hegel,* Frederick C. Beiser, ed.

6. For a reading of the *Phenomenology* that emphasizes the master–slave relationship, see (once again) Kojève's *Introduction*.

7. I am basing my reading of Hegel's concept of "recognition" upon Irigaray's discussion of his philosophy in *J'aime à toi*.

8. For a more detailed analysis of the dialectical progression of the Hegelian subject, see Findlay's foreword to the *Phenomenology*.

9. As mentioned earlier, those critics who focus upon the Hegelian notion of "contradiction" to argue that Hegelian thought is, in the final analysis, nontotalizing would obviously disagree with my interpretation. Zizek's *The Sublime Object of Ideology* and Gillian Rose's *Dialectic of Nihilism in Post-Structuralism*

and Law make a very strong case for the argument that Hegelian philosophy is nontotalizing.

10. Allen W. Wood offers a helpful general introduction to the ethical dimension of Hegel's Philosophy of Right in his essay "Hegel's Ethics," in *The Cambridge Companion to Hegel*. Luce Irigaray (*J'aime à toi*) and Genevieve Lloyd (*The Man of Reason: "Male" and "Female" in Western Philosophy*) provide groundbreaking feminist readings of Hegel's gendered conception of ethical relations in the family and civic sphere.

11. For a historicized analysis of Hegel's representations of the female subject, see Seyla Benhabib's chapter "On Hegel, Women and Irony," in *Situating the Self: Gender Community and Postmodernism in Contemporary Ethics*.

12. Naomi Schor argues for the importance of Hegelian theories of the citizen-subject to feminist thought, and particularly to the work of Luce Irigaray, in "French Feminism Is a Universalism," in *Bad Objects: Essays Popular and Unpopular*.

13. My translation of passages from Irigaray's *Speculum: de l'autre femme*.

14. My translation of passages from Irigaray's *J'aime à toi*.

15. *The Princeton Handbook of Poetic Terms*, Alex Preminger, ed.

2

The Social Model of Citizenship: Comte's *A General View of Positivism*

F ew social philosophers exercised as profound an influence on diverse branches of nineteenth-century thought as Auguste Comte. His positivist theories laid the foundations for sociology,[1] the modern empirical sciences, as well as for a more systematic approach to historiography.[2] Although Comte's impact on nineteenth-century culture is widely studied and acknowledged, his work is rarely regarded as elaborating a theory of modern citizenship. Nor has Comte's work been examined side by side with the influential novels of nineteenth-century France that prescribed, albeit through very different means of representation, men's and women's social and political roles in the modern nation-state. I would like to argue that such an analysis of positivist philosophy is not only appropriate, but also essential to understanding Comte's writing and the emerging model of citizenship.

Comte's philosophy, I maintain, provides one of the most systematic elaborations of the rise of what political theorists call "the social model of citizenship." Political theorists and sociologists such as T. H. Marshall[3] and Jacques Donzelot[4] argue that to understand the development of citizenship during the nineteenth century, we must differentiate it from its eighteenth-century manifestations. Marshall's theory of citizenship traces the transition from the "due process" and "political rights" models of citizenship proposed by eighteenth-century republicanism to the model of citizenship based upon caretaking and "social rights" propagated during the nineteenth century. The modern nation-state, he argues, no longer functions only as the guarantor of individual rights. The state begins to be regarded as the protector of the moral and physical health and well-being of the social organism as a whole.[5] The transition from a political rights model of citizenship to one that is concerned with the welfare of social groups—the most basic and important of these being the nuclear family—also marks the transition from a masculine model of citizenship to an ambisexual one. Whereas, as Carole Pateman illustrates, the older rights model of citizenship arguably assumed a male/universal citizen-subject,[6] a model of citizenship organized around an ethics of caretaking, sympathy, and social welfare takes on feminine cultural characteristics.

Comte's elaboration of such a "social model of citizenship" enables us to explore the following questions: Why and how do women become regarded as exemplary citizen-subjects in nineteenth-century French culture? What are the implications of the centralization of women's citizenship functions for the masculine models of either limited or universal manhood suffrage that were so heatedly debated in France during the nineteenth century?[7] How do nineteenth-century texts justify regarding women as the repositories of civic virtue while continuing to deprive them of political power?[8] In raising and proposing answers to these questions, Comte's work provides an optimal point of entrance into the debates regarding the nature of citizenship that shaped nineteenth-century French literature, society, and culture.

FROM A SINGLE DIALECTICAL (POSITIVIST) MODEL OF CITIZENSHIP TO A DOUBLE DIALECTICAL MODEL

Between the years 1851 and 1854, Auguste Comte wrote *A General View of Positivism* in order to correct what he considered to be misreadings of his *Course of Positive Philosophy*.[9] This earlier work had been published as a series of public lectures, delivered between the years 1830 and 1842, that provided an exposition of positivist philosophy. Comte explains that what needs to be corrected is not so much the "sociology" proposed by the *Course* as the way in which that book had been misunderstood as neglecting social feeling, sympathy, and imagination in favor of abstract reasoning:

> In the following series of systematic essays upon Positivism the essential principles of the doctrine are first considered. . . . It will enable any competent reader to assure himself that the new general doctrine aims at something more than satisfying the Intellect; that it is in reality quite as favorable to Feeling and even to Imagination. (*A General View*, 1)

To defend positivist philosophy, Comte finds it necessary to transform it. I would like to propose that what is at work in Comte's interjection of feeling and imagination into his former rationalist sociology is a process of converting a single dialectical understanding of historical inquiry presented in the *Course* into the double dialectical one we find in the *General View*. Whereas the single dialectical model charts the rational progress of human knowledge across the ages, the double dialectical model outlines the interaction among social groups who are assigned a division of faculties between feeling and reason. Let us examine this transition in Comte's model of citizenship, a shift that, I would argue, is symptomatic of the political and social transformations of nineteenth-century France. The theory of knowledge proposed in the *Course*, although divided into a total of twelve stages, can be reduced to three main historical periods that develop according to a linear and progressive logic.

Comte asserts that human knowledge begins with a theological stage characterized by blind faith in supernatural powers and theocratic authority. This stage is manifested politically in the doctrine of the divine right of kings. From the Renaissance to the Enlightenment, Comte argues, social knowledge grows increasingly rational. It arrives at a metaphysical stage that negates the previous historical epoch by questioning both divine and absolute human authority. The last and ultimate stage of human knowledge dialectically negates and incorporates both blind faith and skeptical reason to arrive at a "positive stage." During this final historical period, Comte wishfully projects, positivist philosophers triumph over rationalist skeptics by discovering the true workings of society through close empirical observation. They also triumph over the blind faith of the theological stage of civilization by trusting only sensory evidence of their analytical abilities. This positivist phase of civilization, understood as the partial negation and selective incorporation of the former two phases, enables sociologists to lead society toward a newfound intellectual and spiritual strength.

Comte's early description of positivism assumes an empirico-rational subject: a kind of evaluating consciousness that observes and makes predictions about the physical and social world. It is this version of positivism—namely, positivism understood as a dialectical historical process that yields objective knowledge about society—that has so profoundly influenced science and social thought during the nineteenth and twentieth centuries. Comte's positivist philosophy elicited both criticism and praise. On the one hand, critics maintained that Comte left imagination and feeling out of the picture of social progress.[10] On the other hand, those who felt Comte's philosophy justified their empiricist methods were quite pleased with its systematic defense of close observation and its faith in the human ability to acquire true, factual knowledge.

Comte himself, however, was less than satisfied with empiricism. In response to criticisms of his positivist philosophy, he attempted to transform that theory into a double dialectical model of social relations among human communities that are perceived as opposites: women and men; the working and the middle classes. This new elaboration of positivism proposes a synthesis of intellectual knowledge and concrete social relations that transforms what was essentially a theory of knowledge into a political theory of subject-citizenship:

> Positivism consists essentially of a Philosophy and a Polity. These can never be dissevered; the former being the basis, and the latter the end of one comprehensive system, in which our intellectual faculties and our social sympathies are brought into close correlation with each other. (*A General View*, 1)

His new version of positivist philosophy, Comte insists, represents not so much a radical break with his former theory as a supplementation of it. To his former positivist epistemology—which he now calls the "philosophical" component of positivism—Comte adds a theory of civic identity, which he calls "a polity." The positivist "philosophy" and "polity" combine in a particular kind of relationship. The philosophy serves as "the basis" of positivism, providing a means of obtaining and validating knowledge. The polity constitutes "the end" of positivism, using that knowledge to create a better social order.[11] To argue that the philosophy and polity of positivism "can never be dissevered," Comte must bring "into close correlation with each other" our rational "intellectual faculties" and "our social sympathies." The qualities that Comte wishes to combine in his revision of subject-citizenship have a profoundly gendered history.

Since the eighteenth century, the division of spheres depended upon associating women with natural feelings of sympathy and men with rational faculties. Eighteenth-century texts tended to argue that the domestic sphere, and particularly the family, provided the best, if not the only legitimate, social space in which women could exercise their ethical influence.[12] Comte, however, extends women's influence to the public sphere. This augmentation of women's social and political power is not altogether unique. As Denise Riley explains in *Am I That Name*, by the nineteenth century women were associated with the idea of "the social," which is precisely what Comte means by the term "social sympathies."[13] Conversely, men were associated with the rational discussions that took place in the public sphere, where they exercised what Comte calls their "intellectual faculties."

As noted, Comte's earlier elaboration of positivism described the progression of abstract knowledge and the evolution of government without accounting for the existence of social and ethical feelings, which were assuming a prominent place in nineteenth-century culture. Comte's revision of his earlier positivism attempts to bring the separate spheres together into a new ambisexual model of citizenship. In his civic theory, women's sympathies are defined through the exclusion of the rationality exercised by men in the public sphere. Conversely, men's rationality is defined through the exclusion of the sympathy exercised by women in the private and social spheres. In effect, Comte wishes to transform a society governed by rational male citizen-subjects—the kind of society implicitly mapped out by his first theory of positivism—into a more sympathetic society ruled by both women and men.

Defending positivist philosophy as representative of, rather than the exception to, this cultural trend, Comte proposes to

> show, in spite of prejudices which exist very naturally on this point, that Positivism is eminently calculated to call the Imaginative faculties into exercise. It is by these faculties that the unity of human nature is most distinctly represented: they are themselves intellectual, but their field lies principally in our moral nature, and the result of their operation is to influence the active powers. (*A General View,* 5)

Once again, in wishing to intertwine imaginative, emotive, and rational faculties in his revision of subject-citizenship, Comte relies upon older, eighteenth-century models of citizenship. As we recall, Rousseau's works dialectically combined rationality and social feeling in a masculine subject.[14] By the nineteenth century, however, this combination of qualities in the masculine and supposedly universal citizen-subject had split into a division of labor between sympathetic women, charged with an ethics of caretaking, and rational men, charged with systematizing and implementing such an ethics.[15] Comte's philosophy contributes to the creation of this new ambisexual model of social and political ethics.

In his theory, Comte announces, "the intellectual movement and the social crisis will be brought continually into close connection with each other. The primary object, then, of Positivism is twofold: to generalize our scientific conceptions and to systematize the art of social life" (2–3). Comte's description of positivist objectives begins by relying upon a division of labor between women and men that positions the sexes in a complementary relationship. Bourgeois men must generalize scientific conceptions, while bourgeois women must systematize the art of social life by inculcating, in both private and public spheres, the right kind of mores.[16] By combining these two gendered functions in a new ambisexual civic domain, Comte hopes to create a complete, both ethical and rational, society.

CLASSES OF CITIZEN-SUBJECTS

Comte's contribution to nineteenth-century social and political thought, however, consists not only of providing a dialectical model of social progress, which Hegel had already done more systematically. More important, Comte shows why social progress cannot be understood only in terms of masculine, bourgeois, and rationalist codes: that is, abstract models of citizenship that neglect the complex interactions among different social groups. Consequently, Comte reasons, social theory must also account for the valuable cultural contributions of women and the working classes:

> Whether we regard its intellectual character or its social objects, it is certain that Positivism must look elsewhere [than bourgeois men] for support. It will find a welcome in those classes only whose good sense has been left unimpaired by our vicious system of education, and whose generous sympathies are allowed to develop themselves freely. It is among women, therefore, and among the working classes that the heartiest supporters of the new doctrine will be found. It is intended, indeed, ultimately for all classes of society. (3–4)

Comte's earlier work represented the subject as implicitly bourgeois and male—reliant, in fact, upon the kind of high education that he now considers counterproductive to the exercise of civic sympathy. In his revision, the working classes and women come to exemplify "the universal civic subject(s)" precisely because they are excluded from institutionalized knowledge. What renders women and the working classes universal is not their ability to represent "mankind" but, on the contrary, their unique behavior.

By placing civic leadership in the hands of those who are least educated, Comte revises not only the argument of his mentor and precursor, Henri de Saint-Simon, but also that of most nineteenth-century social philosophers.[17] Comte's writing intervenes at a moment in French history when even the most utopian of social thinkers were keenly aware of social divisions that invalidated universal ethical and political theories. Even utopian socialists such as Saint-Simon, whom Comte admired and imitated, took into account and attempted to attenuate class divisions. Nonetheless, Saint-Simon's ideal was organized by hierarchical principles even while striving for "cooperative commonwealth."

Believing that intellectuals represented the best human qualities, Saint-Simon organized his hierarchical society into three interacting classes: the intellectual elite whose function was to inculcate the right morals and education in the rest of society; the leaders of industry who were charged with administrative affairs and economic production; and the working classes who, in compensation for their work, would be led toward material and moral improvement by the intelligentsia. Being aware of the problems of placing civic power in the hands of an intellectual elite, Comte rejects the central premise of Saint-Simon's version of socialism. More specifically, he disagrees with the assumption that the educated upper-middle-class male elite epitomizes the best elements of human nature. Not only does Comte argue that education can corrupt moral sympathies, but also he founds his alternative social system upon historical interpretations that differ from those of Saint-Simon.

Comte feels disappointed by the course of French history. On the one hand, he distances himself from the ultimate tyranny of revolutionary democratic principles. On the other hand, he criticizes the undemocratic nature of the July Monarchy, which promised a representative government but in practice extended the vote only to a slightly larger number of propertied men. The solution to these political extremes, Comte suggests, is to place the moral leadership of society neither in the hands of the masses nor in the hands of a propertied elite. Instead, society must attain a dialectical relationship between the working and middle classes that gives the appropriate kind of power to both. He observes,

> The period between 1830 and 1848 may be regarded as a natural pause in the political movement.... Thanks to the instinctive sense and vigor of our working classes, the reactionist leanings of the Orleanist government, which had become hostile to the purpose for which it was originally instituted, have at last brought about the final abolition of monarchy in France. (76–77)

According to Comte, the Orleanist government was not able to stifle all republican opposition by means of repression. Nor was it able to accommodate class-based conflicts by creating an egalitarian society. Comte believes that Louis-Philippe d'Orléan's "bourgeois monarchy" culminated in the violent revolution of 1848 and crumbled because it could not govern all of society. That is to say, the July Monarchy could neither incorporate the working classes into its own structure through democratic representation nor could it negate the power of this excluded group. The lesson of 1848, Comte indicates, was that the people and the revolutionary spirit best represent history's dialectical movement:

> Viewed negatively, the principle of Republicanism sums up the first phase of the Revolution. It precludes the possibility of recurrence to Royalism, which, ever since the second half of the reign of Louis XIV, has been the rallying point of all reactionist tendencies. Interpreting the principle in a

positive sense, we may regard it as a direct step towards the final regenera-
tion of society. (76–77)

According to Comte's political logic, however, the French Revolution,
and particularly its most extreme phase under Robespierre's Reign of
Terror (1791–1793), represents only the first stage, or a first negation of
absolutist principles, in the dynamics of social history. The French Revolution represented the negation of absolutist principles by placing power
(at least in theory) in the hands of the people. At the same time, the Revolution also incorporated absolutist repressive tactics to maintain power.
Why does republicanism, then, represent an improvement over monarchy? Comte explains,

> By consecrating all human forces of whatever kind to the general service of
> the community, republicanism recognizes the doctrine of subordinating
> Politics to Morals. . . . The direct tendency, then, of the French Republic is
> to sanction the fundamental principle of Positivism, the preponderance,
> namely, of Feeling over Intellect and Activity. (78)

By claiming that republicanism is more progressive than either absolutist (the Bourbons) or bourgeois (Louis-Philippe) monarchies, Comte
attempts to transform what he considers to be an individualist model of
citizenship into a collectivist one that is concerned with the welfare of
diverse communities. According to Comte, monarchy subordinates "Morals" to "Politics." In his estimation, morality represents the one code that
should be followed by all human communities. Conversely, politics represents the machinations by which some individuals acquire power over
others.

The interplay between power and ethics sets monarchy and democracy
in an inverse relationship. Monarchy begins with universalist ethical principles—the supposedly unquestioned divine laws that govern society—
only to end up splintering its supposed universal ethical codes into competing political interests. Consequently, what begins as an ethics ends up
as a politics. Conversely, republican democracy begins with the nonuniversalist recognition that the interests of the masses and of the privileged few are, or at least can be, at odds. For this reason, republican theory
contends that the elite should not govern the masses. Comte transforms
the nonuniversalist politics of republican theory into a universalist ethics.
He argues that, in fact, the people should govern the elite. While the elite
may still be motivated by the competitive individualism of its class, the
people are concerned with collective well-being. Hence, in place of a
society divided by competing class interests, Comte institutes a society
that serves the interests of a truly universal class—the working class—
which represents all classes.

Why is the working-class subject better qualified than the bourgeois subject to provide civic leadership in society? "[I]ndependently of their intrinsic merits, whether intellectual or moral," Comte contends, "the necessities of their daily life serve to impress them with respect for the great rules of morality, which in most cases were framed for their own protection" (151). The working-class subject is a better civic subject, according to Comte, not because of natural differences, but because of his class position. The need to have enough food, clothing, and shelter compels him to depend upon co-citizens, to share resources with others, to exercise civic sympathy. What the working-class subject may lack in education, he makes up in social collaboration.

Because positivism privileges feeling over reason, Comte argues, "public opinion will soon be convinced that the work of organizing society on republican principles is one which can only be performed by the new philosophy" (79). To claim that republicanism and positivism arise from the same assumptions, however, does not necessarily prove that they follow the same logic. In the third chapter of *A General View of Positivism*, entitled "Its Actions on the People," Comte identifies the conceptual similarities between positivist theory and republican citizenship. He goes so far as to demonstrate that only positivism can provide a historical account of the emergence of democratic citizenship. In so doing, he starts with the same argument he mentioned at the beginning of his work: namely, that his second "sympathetic" version of positivist philosophy is founded upon and helps transform the first "rationalist" one. A sympathetic notion of citizenship cannot afford to ignore the interests of any class. It must be produced through the dialectical interactions of all classes. Consequently, the working class can become the standard of universal citizenship not only by negating the individualism and rationalism that Comte attributes to the bourgeoisie, but also by incorporating such principles.

"The working class," Comte declares, "is better qualified than any other for understanding, and still more for sympathizing with the highest truth of morality, *though it may not be able to give them a systematic form*" (151, my emphasis). The philosopher limits the power of the working classes to incorporate bourgeois reasoning into republican sympathy (151). How can the qualities of the bourgeois educated subject and his negation—namely, the uneducated worker—be brought together to form a better society? Comte offers the following solution:

> And the principal means of realizing it will be the formation of an alliance between philosophers and the working classes. . . . The direct object of their combined action will be to set in motion the force of Public Opinion. . . . It is in this beneficial influence that we shall find the surest guarantee for morality; for domestic and even for personal morality. (153)

According to Comte's dialectical logic, the "combined action" of the bourgeois and working-class subjects does not mean that these two classes, defined as sociopolitical opposites, unite to produce a new class composed of both sympathetic and intellectual civic subjects. Like his mentor, Saint-Simon, Comte postulates a division of labor between the working and middle classes that not only preserves their differences, but also requires those distinctions to forge a new social order.

The affiliation between working-class and bourgeois men, however, leaves something out: the social roles of women. Women, as we recall, infuse the social order with domestic and personal morality. While dividing men in terms of class, he imagines that bourgeois women represent a universal class whose natural characteristics are shared by all of its members. How does Comte's philosophy move from this initial contract between groups of men to a society that depends upon the participation of women?

At each step of its dialectical process, Comte's positivism shows both an improvement over a previous stage and a lack that necessitates the progression toward a new phase. His depiction of the role of the working classes in the French Revolution generates a need for a different kind of civic subject. By themselves, the working classes could only move society to the next step of its progressive dynamics. As we recall, this step traced the movement from one political extreme (absolute monarchy) to another (chaotic democracy). Moreover, according to Comte, the very social conditions that produce the sympathetic civic feelings of the working classes can also have the opposite effect, of encouraging self-serving emotions. In chapter IV of *A General View,* entitled "The Influence of Positivism upon Women," Comte explains why a society governed by men remains imperfect, thereby justifying the intervention of women in the civic sphere:

> The moral constitution of man consists of something more than Intellect and Activity. These are represented in the constitution of society by the philosophic body and the proletariat. But besides these there is Feeling. . . . Now the alliance between philosophers and working men, which has been just described, however imperfectly it may be realized, does not represent the element of Feeling with sufficient distinctness and prominence. . . . [In] their case its source is not sufficiently pure or deep to sustain them in the performance of their duty. (227)

The problem with the sympathies of the working classes, Comte suggests, is that they are grounded in culture, not nature. Assuming nature to offer a more stable foundation for ethical behavior than changing social and economic circumstances, he declares that "A more spontaneous and more perennial spring of inspiration must be found" (227). The source of such a "spring," Comte maintains, is women.

To explain this assumption, he proceeds to redefine the two kinds of masculine subjects he has described so far—bourgeois and working-class men—in terms of their difference from the naturally sympathetic and universal female subject. The feminine subject displaces working-class men in Comte's argument as the standard of civic virtue:

> Intercourse with the working classes will be of the greatest benefit to him; but even this is not enough to compensate the defects of a life devoted to speculation. The sympathies of the people again, though stronger and more spontaneous than those of the philosopher, are, in most cases, less pure and not so lasting. From the pressure of daily necessities it is difficult for them to maintain the same disinterested character. (277)

Comte claims that the feelings of working-class men are based on the nature of their social needs and interdependency. Their impoverishment, crowded living conditions, and large families lead working men to collaborate with one another in a way that bourgeois men do not. He believes, however, that this cooperation remains in important respects self-serving. Working class men grant a favor out of economic need and with the expectation that it will be returned. Only women's natural virtue is sufficiently disinterested to meet Comte's standards. It is worth noting that even when he most forcefully proposes a feminine subject as the standard of citizenship, Comte simultaneously assumes that a masculine subject constitutes the implicit norm of humanity. Interaction with both the working classes and with women is ultimately meant to be of the "greatest benefit to him," the bourgeois man.

By shaping social groups and forces for the benefit of bourgeois men, Comte places women in the same paradoxical position he put working-class men. On the one hand, women constitute the better representatives of subject-citizenship. On the other hand, the whole notion of citizenship revolves around improving the bourgeois male subject. At this point in Comte's narrative, however, the marginalization of the working classes and particularly of women remains implicit. What matters most in this first phase of a double dialectic is that women have something to offer to citizenship that men of all classes lack:

> Thus, in the alliance which has been here proposed as necessary for social reorganization [between philosophers and the working classes], Feeling, the most influential part of human nature, has not been adequately represented. . . . On this, as well as on other grounds, it is indispensable that Women be associated in the work of regeneration as soon as its tendencies and conditions can be explained to them. (277–278)

In making the transition from a rational and culturally sympathetic civic sphere to a naturally sympathetic one, Comte begins to outline the

gynocentric loop of the double dialectics of subject-citizenship. Consequently, in contrast to Hegel, Comte does not argue for the incorporation
and subordination of feminine feeling to masculine reason. He proposes
instead "the subordination of intellect to social feeling: a subordination
which we find directly represented in the womanly type of character,
whether regarded in its personal or social relations" (5). As noted, the
feminine subject—sometimes in collaboration with the working-class male
subject—becomes a better, and presumably more modern, model of subject-citizenship than the rational bourgeois man. Comte goes so far as to
declare that "it is from the feminine aspect only that human life, whether
individually or collectively considered, can really be comprehended as a
whole" (4–5). To view women as representatives of the human "whole,"
however, does not exclude viewing femininity as part of a dialectical process, motivated by mutually negating masculine and feminine qualities.
Just as Hegel viewed masculinity as representative of the human in contrast to a negated version of femininity, so Comte views women as the
human standard only when their social roles are understood in a chiasmic
relation to those of men. Representing each sex as the negative of the other
sex obviously does not entail doing away with gender categories. Rather
than displacing gender distinctions, Comte's model of citizenship renders
them less hierarchical.

Why must the citizen-subject of positivist philosophy be, at least initially, female? Comte explains the gender of citizenship in terms of common perceptions of femininity: "To the Positivist the object of Morals is
to make our sympathetic instincts preponderate as far as possible over the
selfish instincts; social feelings over personal feelings" (101). This conception of women as governed primarily by unselfish sympathetic instincts
is based upon cultural ideals suggesting how nineteenth-century women
should behave. Such a view is also established conceptually, by means of
the implicit negation of the selfish motivations associated with a masculine subject. Only this exclusion of masculinity from civic ethics enables
Comte to universalize the social identity of the feminine subject:

> Full and free expansion of the benevolent emotions is made the first condi-
> tion of individual and social well being, since these emotions are at once the
> sweetest to experience, and are the only feelings which can find expression
> simultaneously in all. (103)

In an apparently contradictory logical move, Comte maintains both that
women best epitomize sympathetic feelings and that such emotions, being "the sweetest to experience," can be found "simultaneously in all."

Why does Comte adopt this seemingly contradictory position? Because
he wishes to show that the inculcation of social sympathies by women is

a natural and effortless process. Such education would not dramatically change human nature, only enhance its best and most general characteristics. Moreover, by positing simultaneously that social sympathies are common to all humans and require feminine conditioning, Comte transforms a static model of the citizen-subject (epitomized by women) into a dynamic social and moral system that produces sympathetic citizen-subjects of both sexes. In order to accomplish this task, he proposes,

> There are three successive stages of morality answering to the three principal stages of human life; the personal, the domestic, and the social stage. The succession represents the gradual training of the sympathetic principle; it is drawn out step by step by a series of affections which, as it diminishes in intensity, increases in dignity. This series forms our best resource in attempting as far as possible to reach the normal state; subordination of self-love to social feeling. (104)

Once again, the end goal of Comte's version of citizenship is already presupposed as its enabling premise. In order for individuals to subordinate self-love to social feelings, other-regarding sympathies must already be assumed to be a "normal state." At the same time, the gap between the premise and the conclusion of Comte's argument must be bridged through the women's intervention in the civic sphere. As we have seen, Comte postulates that women, as individuals, are the natural representatives of the sympathetic principle on a personal level. Through their influence upon the domestic and social spheres, society by and large can be "drawn out step by step by a series of affections" that aim at the "subordination of self-love to social feeling."

Furthermore, assuming that the further we move away from the source of sympathetic subject-citizenship—namely, personal interactions with women—the weaker their affective influence upon society becomes, Comte argues that the modern nuclear family is the most important conduit of social feeling for society by and large. That is, he regards the family as the smallest social unit regulated by feminine principles. Pursuing this line of reasoning, Comte moves to the next step of dialectical thinking as follows:

> These are the two extremes in the scale of human affections; but between them is an intermediate degree, namely domestic attachment, and it is on this that the solution of the great moral problem depends. The love of his family leads Man out of his original state of Self-love and enables him to attain finally a sufficient measure of Social love. (104)

Love, and particularly familial love, constitutes the middle term of a dialectical process. This process first negates self-regarding masculine

reasoning by valorizing opposite qualities, namely, other-regarding feminine feeling. The narrative then proceeds to negate the particularity of
domestic feeling by transforming it into the more abstract and universal
notion of "social love." By means of this process, "social love" represents
the negation and selective incorporation of both abstract reasoning and
domestic attachment. The outcome of this double negation of individualist reason is a conception of civic love that combines the abstraction and
universality of rational thought with the affective specificity of domestic
relations. It should be noted that Comte's doubling of the positivist dialectic modifies the commonplace view of the family as a kind of complementary union between women and men. Describing the family unit in
terms of the dialectical interactions between male and female subjects,
Comte produces a version of civic citizenship that is androgynous in the
sense of being *neither* male nor female, but a partial negation of both genders.

We may now ask, how does Comte's ethical model of the family, and
particularly of feminine subjects, inculcate the right kind of moral and
civic values into society by and large? First, for Comte, the modern nuclear
family exemplifies, by its very existence, the right kind of values. The new
heterosexual couple marries out of individuated and selfless emotion, not
to make self-interested political alliances:

> The heart cannot throw off its original selfishness, without the aid of some
> complete and enduring affection. And conjugal love, concentrated as it is
> upon one object exclusively, is more enduring and more complete than any
> other. From personal experience of strong love we rise by degrees to sincere
> affection for all mankind. (262)

Only the ideal of monogamous love, propagated by women, can begin
to offset selfish desires, especially on the part of men. Similarly, according to Comte, it follows that if love is to be genuine and pure, it must not
only be monogamous, but also selfless. Assuming physical desire to be
impelled by selfish motives—namely, the satisfaction of personal desire—
Comte reasons that only its negation would constitute modern marriage
as an ethical relationship:

> Thus the theory of marriage, as set forward by the Positivist, becomes to-
> tally independent of any physical motive. It is regarded by him as the most
> powerful instrument of moral education; and therefore as the basis of pub-
> lic or individual welfare. (287)

As we have seen, according to Comte's understanding of sexual relations, women represent the ideal citizen-subjects. Since Comte accepts the

commonplace notion that bourgeois women are unmoved by physical desires, then according to his dialectical logic, men are motivated by physical drives that can be kept in check only by women. As the mother–wife becomes both the model and the reproducer of individuated love, she acquires greater power both inside and outside the family:

> As a mother, no less than as a wife, her position will be improved by Positivism. She will have, almost exclusively, the direction of household education. Public education given subsequently, will be but a systematic development of that which has been previously given at home. (268)

Comte is aware that, by portraying mothers as the perfect models of subject-citizenship, he is overturning long-standing cultural assumptions. The view that women are anything but fit to educate children, and particularly boys, was most seductively articulated by Jean-Jacques Rousseau in his educational treatise *Emile, ou de l'éducation*. Women's frail and dependent nature, the argument goes, can only produce a nation of weak and effeminate male citizens. Beginning with this premise, Rousseau and other eighteenth- and nineteenth-century social theorists argued for the separation of school-age children, and especially of boys, from their mothers. Napoleon's system of education for boys implemented a social system based on the exclusion of women from the civic sphere and on the separation between women and men that had its roots in eighteenth-century thought. This model of the division of spheres aims to produce a masculine version of citizenship where women have little or no influence upon the civic order. Obviously, Comte sought to reverse this model of citizenship. To displace this older model, he had to offer compelling reasons for expanding the cultural influence of women both within and outside of the private sphere:

> There are strong prejudices against entrusting the education of children to mothers: prejudices springing from the revolutionary spirit of modern times. Since the close of the Middle Ages, the tendency has been to place the intellect above the heart. We have neglected the moral side of education, and have given importance to the intellectual side. (268)

To justify placing civic responsibilities in the hands of women, Comte counters two further powerful arguments against it. First, he wishes to reverse the priorities between the impartial reasoning traditionally attributed to bourgeois men (which was viewed as a prerequisite for citizenship that women lacked) and the emotions or passions attributed to women (which were viewed as an impediment to impartial reasoning and disqualified women from participating in the public sphere). Comte argues that the assumptions behind this model of masculine citizenship are inherently flawed. The rational faculties represented by bourgeois men, rather than encouraging impartial judgment, cause each individual to act on behalf of his own rational self-interest. By way of contrast, the emotions ascribed to women lead them to acquire universal social sympathies that transcend egoistic impulses. Far from interjecting disorder into the civic sphere, as many eighteenth- and nineteenth-century theorists and politicians argued, women would actually contribute to the creation of a better and more orderly society based upon the cooperation of diverse social groups.

The second cultural commonplace Comte must contend with is the assumption, once again propagated by many republican politicians, that women are politically reactionary and dogmatically religious. On the contrary, Comte maintains, women are socially progressive. Progress, in his estimation, does not signify the elimination of class differences or the complete democratization of society. Comte proposes instead a more Romantic vision of social progress, whereby different classes subordinate political group interests to collective morals:

> At present the general feeling amongst them [women] is antipathy to the Revolution. They dislike the destructive character which the Revolution necessarily exhibited in its first phase. . . . All their social sympathies are given to the Middle Ages. . . . [T]he real ground of their predilection . . . is that, being morally the purest portion of Humanity, they venerate Catholicism, as the only system which has upheld the principle of subordinating Politics to Morals. . . . It is a complete mistake to charge women with being retrograde on account of these feelings of regret which are most honorable to them. (229–230)

Once women are placed in charge of education and at the moral center of the family and civic sphere, it is no longer feasible to argue that they should remain uneducated. Rousseau could maintain that women only need a very limited education in domestic work precisely because his theory of citizenship did not entrust women with important civic functions. Given his different social objectives, Comte could not afford to propose the same kind of policy for women. In order for women to be competent in their civic duties, Comte argues, their education should be almost identical to that of men:

> Since the vocation assigned by our theory to women is that of educating others, it is clear that the educational system which we have proposed . . . for the working classes, applies to them as well as to the other sex with very slight alterations. (278)

According to Comte's own premises concerning the effects of excessive knowledge, neither women nor the working classes should be educated exactly like bourgeois men. Such an education, as we remember, develops analytical faculties at the expense of moral ones. Instead of proposing that women pursue advanced education, Comte states that they should acquire a basic intellectual training intended to enhance their social sympathies and deepen their historical knowledge. Consequently, according to Comte, both women and men "need historical instruction as a basis for the systematization of moral truth" (278). To develop the requisite analytical abilities for decision-making, "both should alike pass through the scientific training which prepares the way for social studies" (278). This training necessitates that both women and men obtain the same primary and secondary education.

"The only department with which they [women] need not concern themselves," Comte cautions, "is what is called professional education. . . . In all other respects women, philosophers, and working men will receive the same education" (278–279). This qualification indicates that women must remain different from men if they want to remain good citizen-subjects. They should not have access to advanced education or enter the professions. Furthermore, they must remain external to the political sphere. Along with other political theorists, Comte represents this restriction of women not only as beneficial to society by and large, but also as desired by women themselves:

> They [women] care little for metaphysical theories of society in which human happiness is made to consist in a continual exercise of political rights; for political rights, however attractively presented, will always fail to interest them. . . . They will wish all success to philosophers and workmen when they see them endeavoring to transform political disputes into social compacts, and proving that they have greater regard for duties than for rights. (231)

Because Comte's double dialectics bestows identity on women by excluding the rational/public identity of men, women must remain outside of the political domain if they are to remain feminine and thus capable of exercising control over the social sphere. Women's exclusion from the public arena is justified in terms of a voluntaristic logic: women, by nature, want to be excluded as a group. Their exclusion is also justified by the dialectical interaction between the gendered political concepts of duties and rights. Since women are sympathetic civic subjects, they must serve as the upholders of social duties for other citizens and the state. Likewise, since men are the opposite of women, they must serve as repositories of individual rights as delineated by the *Declaration of the Rights of Man and Citizen*.

This exclusion of women from individual rights in the public sphere, which reduces them to the status of venerated noncitizens, begins the second, androcentric loop of the chiasmus. In the public sphere, it is women who assume a cultural identity only by representing the negation of the positive identity of men. When men are defined as political subjects, then women are defined as nonpolitical subjects. Comte summarizes the double dialectics of gender as follows:

> The social mission of woman in the Positive system follows as a natural consequence from the qualities peculiar to her nature. In the most essential attribute of the human race, the tendency to place the social above personal feeling, she is undoubtedly superior to men. . . . But these qualities do not involve the possession of political power, which some visionaries have claimed for women, though without their own consent. In that which is the great object of human life, they [women] are superior to men; but in the various means of attaining that object they are undoubtedly inferior. In all kinds of force, whether physical, intellectual, or practical, it is certain that Man surpasses Woman, in accordance with a general law which prevails throughout the animal kingdom. (234)

To chart out an androgynous model of citizenship, Comte must privilege women over men in some respects and men over women in others. By nature, women provide the ethics of citizenship; men, however, actually carry out its functions.

At this point, Comte's model of citizenship begins to duplicate the workings of older, masculine models. Like them, positivism argues for the very division of spheres it took such pains to displace and complicate. By stating that "we find it the case in every phase of human society that women's life is essentially domestic, public life being confined to men" (235), Comte deprives women of much of the civic power and influence he just granted them. Consequently, as Riley suggests, the nineteenth-century creation of "the social" sphere, situated on the intersection between the old private and public spheres, gives women civic power with one hand while refusing them political power with the other. According to Riley, this double gesture observes the following logic: "'Women' are overwhelmingly sociological and therefore, given these new definitions, not political entities; indeed, the suffrage struggles grind on in vain during these decades, as emancipation is endlessly deferred."[18]

THE ANDROGYNOUS MODEL OF SUBJECT-CITIZENSHIP AND THE LIMITS OF POLITICAL REPRESENTATION

Comte's description of masculine subjects as defined by the exclusion of feminine sympathies and of feminine subjects as defined by the exclusion of rational abilities and political power obscures some of the complexities of his earlier definition of the social. As we recall, Comte had described the social as an androgynous space, neither masculine nor feminine, which is governed by citizen-subjects who have already sublated gender contradictions. If we take Comte's later, binary definition of gender literally, however, then women would not be able to exercise the civic duties he upholds. Nor could they obtain the education that Comte had found necessary for their intellectual development. By extension, then, men would not be capable of acquiring the social sympathies required by his polity.

Having painted himself into a logical corner, Comte carries his argument to its conclusion. He suggests that, in the end, no social group is ethically capable of exercising political power. Consequently, at the conclusion of his book, he argues that bourgeois men, the working classes, and women should all be disqualified from active citizenship because, as his theory has demonstrated, all three groups have major flaws that preclude them from governing society. Having differentiated women from men by means of women's exclusion from political functions, Comte proceeds to state that this exclusion did not distinguish women after all: "[T]he social position of women is in this respect similar to that of philosophers and the working classes. . . . Philosophers are excluded from political power by the same fatality as women, although they are apt to think that their intellectual eminence gives them a claim to it" (236).

What is the "fatality" that excludes bourgeois philosophers, the working classes, and bourgeois women from politics? Comte explains: "Were our material wants more easily satisfied, the influence of intellect would be less impeded than it is by the practical business of life" (236). In other words, as he stated earlier, men's intellect tends to serve individual material needs. "But, on this hypothesis, women would have a better claim to govern than philosophers," he adds, since he has shown that women would not be governed by the same selfish motives. Consequently, Comte concludes, "A life of thought is a more evident disqualification for the government of the world even than a life of feeling. . . . With all its pretensions, intellectual force is not in itself more moral than material force [attributed to the working classes]" (236).

What is the extent of women's and men's influence after this process of disqualification? Apparently, very minimal. According to Comte, it is up to the wealthy to continue ruling society: "Our material necessities are so urgent, that those who have the means of providing for them will always be the possessors of power" (238). In stating that the wealthy have political power, Comte believes that he is only depicting the status quo and projecting how society will continue to function. "Power," he maintains, "power, that is, which controls action without persuading the will, has two perfectly distinct sources, numbers and wealth" (237). Comte is not making the moral claim that plutocracy is superior to democracy. He only expresses his sense of resignation at not being able to offer a viable alternative to plutocracy. Despite the necessity of plutocratic rule in government, however, Comte suggests that it is still by means of the interactions of the three classes whose roles he has elaborated that society will develop toward greater civic and moral perfection. Behind the scenes of political representation, as it were, bourgeois men, the working classes, and women would govern society by means of the following division of labor:

> On philosophers rests the duty of giving logical coherence to this principle, and saving it from sophistical attacks. Its practical working depends upon the proletariat class, without whose aid it would almost always be evaded. But to maintain it in all its purity, as an inspiration that needs neither argument nor compulsion, is the work of women only. So constituted, the alliance of the three classes will be the foreshadowed image of the normal state to which Humanity is tending. It will be the living type of perfect human nature. (238–239)

Comte's "perfect human nature," unfortunately, remains unhelpfully abstract. By defining each class by means of the exclusion of the qualities of the others, it is difficult to see how these three classes can understand each other sufficiently to cooperate. But even more puzzling is Comte's definition of subject-citizenship in terms of three forms of dialectically related social identities that have no concrete duties or rights as active citizens in the public sphere. This disjunction between social and political identity certainly yields a new, and in some ways progressive, ambisexual model of citizenship. Such a model both reflects and anticipates the manner in which nineteenth-century French culture was beginning to regard the civic influence of women and of the working classes.

At the same time, Comte's model of citizenship dangerously and inexplicably severs subjects from political power and representation. This, too, represents a characteristic gesture of nineteenth-century social theory. As Riley explains, "One striking effect of the conceptualizing of this 'social' is its dislocation from the political. The latter takes on an intensified air of privacy and invulnerability, of 'high politics' associated with juridical and governmental power in a restricted manner."[19] In effect, because he wishes to avoid carrying his praise of women's exemplary roles as citizen-subjects to its logical conclusion and grant them equivalent forms of political power to men, Comte follows the opposite strategy. He generalizes a model of citizenship that applies to women during the nineteenth century—defined in terms of domestic and social influence—to classes of men.

Consequently, instead of risking masculinizing women by giving them political power, Comte would rather feminize men by depriving them of it. In so doing, he runs into the very contradiction his definition of citizenship, which was dependent upon a contrast between women and men, attempted to avoid. In the end, he proposes an androgynous model of citizenship that is neither masculine nor feminine but whose existence depends upon the division of spheres. Comte's model of citizenship is not conventionally masculine because it upholds a democratic society without granting men, not even the privileged class of bourgeois men, the right to political representation that had become the staple of political discourse. By the same token, his model of citizenship is also not conventionally feminine because it grants women tremendous power in the public arena via their influence of social policies. Such a chiasmic feminization of masculine models of citizenship and masculinization of feminine models of citizenship, as Balzac's *La Cousine Bette* will illustrate, can only lead to trouble. Let us now explore further the conceptual and cultural contradictions inherent in androgynous models of citizenship that confuse, while at the same time uphold, the division of spheres.

NOTES

1. Lewis A. Coser provides an excellent historical introduction to Comte's sociology in *Masters of Sociological Thought: Ideas in Historical and Social Context*. Raymond Aron explores Comte's sociology in relation to the social philosophies of other major modern thinkers in *Main Currents in Sociological Thought: Montesquieu, Comte, Marx, Tocqueville*.

2. For a critical discussion of Comte's influence on late nineteenth- and early twentieth-century science and epistemology, see Roy Bhaskar's *Reclaiming Reality: A Critical Introduction to Contemporary Philosophy* and several essays on the subject by Anthony Giddens, found in *The Giddens Reader*. In *Poetics of New History*, and particularly in the chapter "The Positivist Paradigm," Philippe Carrard offers an excellent exposition of Comte's influence on the development of more "scientific" positivist methods in historiography.

3. See Marshall's *Class, Status and Citizenship*.

4. See Donzelot's "The Promotion of the Social," in *Economy and Society*. Donzelot's analysis of the emergence of the social is presented in greater detail in *L'Invention du social*.

5. Douglas E. Ashford discusses the state's role in the development of welfare policies during the nineteenth century in *The Emergence of the Welfare States*.

6. Carole Pateman, in *The Sexual Contract* and *The Disorder of Women: Democracy, Feminism and Political Theory*, argues that republican citizenship, based upon a fraternal social contract, necessitates the exclusion of women both conceptually and historically. In the chapter "The Fraternal Social Contract" of the *Disorder of Women*, she states: "The creation of the 'individual' presupposes the division of rational civil order from the disorder of womanly nature. It might thus seem that the civil individual and the body politic made in his image would be

unified. Indeed, they are so presented in liberal theory, but its critics from Rousseau onward argue that the individual and civil society are inherently divided, one from the other and within themselves" (47). We will follow the logic of such divisions, as Comte attempts to create an ideal citizen-subject by combining the qualities of women, bourgeois men, and the working classes, only to end up following the logic of his own theory and excluding all groups from political life.

7. François Furet's *Revolutionary France* offers an excellent introduction to the historical debates and events revolving around the nature and limits of representative government.

8. Several feminist historians analyze the paradoxical citizenship status of women—as repositories of civic virtue who are nevertheless excluded from citizenship—in eighteenth- and nineteenth-century democratic theories and social practice. See, e.g., Jean Bethke's *Public Man, Private Woman: Women in Social and Political Thought*; Christine Fauré's *Democracy without Women: Feminism and the Rise of Liberal Individualism in France*; and Joan Landes's *Women and the Public Sphere in the Age of the French Revolution*.

9. As Arline Reilein Standley explains in *Auguste Comte*, "Taken together, *The System of Positive Polity* (1854), *The Positivist Catechism* (1852), and the *Subjective Synthesis* (1856) spell out . . . Positivism's sociological and educational bases, its religious dogmas and worship, and its social and political structure" (99). *A General View* forms the first volume of the four-volume series *The System of Positive Polity*.

10. Sometimes the praise and criticism came from the same source. For instance, John Stuart Mill, Comte's near-contemporary, expressed admiration for the scientific and systematic nature of Comte's social philosophy but criticized it for its neglect of feeling. See J. S. Mill, *Auguste Comte and Positivism*. For a contemporary critique of Comte's positivism, see F. A. Hayek's *The Counter-Revolution of Science: Studies on the Abuse of Reason*.

11. The deterministic and teleological slants of Comte's social theories have also been criticized by intellectual historians. See, for example, the critique offered by Isaiah Berlin in his article "Historical Inevitability," in *Four Essays on Liberty*, 41–43.

12. Carol Blum provides an illuminating analysis of the role played by gender in the ethics of citizenship, and particularly in Rousseau's model of civic virtue, in *Rousseau and the Republic of Virtue: The Language of Politics in the French Revolution*.

13. In *Am I That Name? Feminism and the Category of "Women" in History*, Riley examines the historical link between the postulation of women's ethics in terms of sympathy and the growth of their political power by taking charge of "caretaking" and philanthropic policies. As she states, "The nineteenth-century 'social' is the reiterated sum of progressive philanthropies, theories of class, of poverty, of degeneration. . . . It is a blurred ground between the old public and private, voiced as a field for intervention, love, and reform by socialists, conservatives, radicals, liberals, and feminists in their different and conjoined ways" (49).

14. See Rousseau's *Emile, ou de l'éducation* and the analysis of Rousseau's formulations of subject-citizenship provided by Joel Schwartz in *The Sexual Politics of Jean-Jacques Rousseau*.

15. See William H. Sewell, Jr.'s "Le Citoyen/la citoyenne: Activity, Passivity, and the Revolutionary Concept of Citizenship," in *The Political Culture of the French Revolution*.

16. As Geneviève Fraisse argues in *Muse de la Raison: La Démocratie exclusive et la différence des sexes,* even the Napoleonic Code, which deprived women, and particularly wives, of legal and political rights, contributed to the ambivalent gesture of enhancing their social power by describing them as the inculcators of social mores.

17. See, once again, Standley's *Auguste Comte*.

18. Riley, *Am I That Name?*, 51.

19. Riley, *Am I That Name?*, 51.

3

Gendered Spheres in Balzac's
La Cousine Bette

During the nineteenth century, the relation of gender to citizenship raised a host of questions whose answers and implications continue to affect our lives. If married women were treated as legal minors under the Napoleonic Code, should single women who were financially independent be treated the same way? Or, because of their social and financial independence, should they be treated differently?[1] Should single women, widows, courtesans, and working women be treated more like women or more like male citizens? What kind of citizen-subjects were they? The fact that these women were economically independent and participated in the public sphere indicated to some that they were more like men and should have the right to vote and govern the nation. Others, however, perceived the existence of these "misfortunate" women as a social threat that might instigate gender subversion and social chaos.[2] If women behaved like or were treated like male citizens, critics argued, the whole foundation of the new nuclear family would be jeopardized. In this chapter, we will explore how and why the existence of "androgynous" women threatened the division of spheres in the nuclear family, and insofar as the nuclear family affected other social institutions, in society by and large.

Balzac's novels enable readers to consider both sides of the debate over women's societal role. To explore this debate, we will begin by examining the ways in which Balzac's *La Cousine Bette* uses the division of spheres to produce the modern nuclear family, which centers around the figure of the mother–wife. According to *La Cousine Bette*, it is only women's new roles as bourgeois mothers—meaning as moral guides, intelligent com-

panions to their husbands, financial managers, and educators of the family—that justify their gender-specific citizenship status: namely, their education and empowerment in the private sphere. At the same time, I will
also show that the division of spheres could not be fully implemented
because not all women were able to carry out the citizenship functions
associated with the bourgeois mother–wife. Nineteenth-century capitalist
society produced different classes of women—working women, widows,
single women, prostitutes, and courtesans—that had to make their living
in the masculine public sphere. This, in turn, disrupted the division of
spheres upheld by many of Balzac's novels and other nineteenth-century
works of popular fiction.

NINETEENTH-CENTURY AESTHETICS
AND THE DIALECTICS OF SUBJECT-FORMATION

How does a focus on Balzac's representation of gender roles contribute
to a literary understanding of his works? I would argue that a close reading of the ways in which Balzac's fiction uses gender to represent and
change the social categories of his time can provide a better understanding of Balzac's depiction of "scenes of private life" than critical analyses
that ignore gender. Traditionally, even those literary critics who expressed
interest in Balzac's representation of private life have overlooked the dimension of gender in Balzac's novels. In so doing, I will argue, they have
imposed a single dialectical model of gendering—which considers female
identity as a lack of male identity—upon what I hope to show constitutes
Balzac's double dialectical model of gender. Let me offer, very briefly,
Georg Lukacs's *The Theory of the Novel* and Fredric Jameson's *The Political
Unconscious* as examples of such single dialectical interpretations of gender. I have selected these texts because they represent two of the most
important literary studies of Balzac's representation of family relations
that follow the logic of the Hegelian dialectic.

In his early work *The Theory of the Novel* (1914–1915), Lukacs argues that
"the novel seeks, by giving form, to uncover and construct the concealed
totality of life."[3] In so doing, he links together by means of a dialectical
process aesthetics and social life. He proposes that the social fragmentation brought about by the growth of capitalist society is critiqued (or negated), represented (or incorporated), and eventually overcome (or
sublated) by the aesthetic totality of realist fiction. Despite its totality,
however, the novel remains a fragile, contradictory, and unstable genre.
In his words, "The danger by which the novel is determined is twofold:
either the fragility of the world may manifest itself so crudely that it will

cancel out its immanence of meaning which the form demands, or else the longing for dissonance to be resolved, affirmed and absorbed into the work may be so great that it will lead to a premature closing of the novel's world, causing the form to disintegrate into disparate, heterogeneous parts" (71). The seemingly finished form of the realist novel—composed of a beginning, body, and resolution—cannot fully conceal the incomplete, contradictory, and contingent nature of the class struggle it aims to represent. Consequently, Lukacs claims, "The fragility of the world may be superficially disguised but it cannot be abolished; consequently this fragility will appear in the novel as unprocessed raw material, whose weak cohesion will have been destroyed" (71–72).

As Lukacs specifies in his later work, *The Historical Novel*, Balzac's realist novel provides the most accurate representation of these historical transitions:

> The great experience of Balzac's youth is the volcanic character of social forces, concealed by the apparent calm of the Restoration period. . . . For these antagonisms exploded in the July Revolution, and the apparent balance between them in Louis Philippe's "bourgeois monarchy" was such an unstable equilibrium that the contradictory and vacillating character of the entire social structure inevitably became the focus of Balzac's conception of history. (84)

Returning to *The Theory of the Novel,* we can discern more clearly the dialectical movements of the realist novel's representation of history as an "unstable equilibrium" of social forces. In a Hegelian move, Lukacs charts the shift from aristocratic to bourgeois-dominated culture in terms of the development of the modern male citizen: "The novel is the art-form of *virile* maturity: this means that the completeness of the novel's world, if seen objectively, is an imperfection, and if subjectively experienced, it amounts to resignation" (71).

In Lukacs's sociohistorical aesthetic, the novel is "virile" because it outlines the dialectical movements of two allegorical forms of masculinity. The first form resembles a proletarian subject who internalizes the class struggle. The second form resembles the male artist who first internalizes and then overcomes class divisions through the self-conscious "objectivity" and coherence of his artistic representation. As in the Hegelian narrative, so in Lukacs's, there are moments of recognition between the intellectual and the proletarian subjects. However, as for Hegel, this mutual recognition quickly becomes one-sided. According to Lukacs's own allegory of subject-formation, only the subject who engages in intellectual (as opposed to manual) labor recognizes himself in the struggles of the proletarian subject and resolves the class struggles of his historical context:

The self-recognition and, with it, self-abolition of subjectivity was called irony by the first theoreticians of the novel, the aesthetic philosophers of early Romanticism. As a formal constituent of the novel form this signifies an interior diversion of the normatively creative subject into a subject as interiority, which opposes power complexes that are alien to it and which strives to imprint the contents of its longing upon the alien world, and a subjectivity which sees through the abstract and, therefore, limited nature of the mutually alien worlds of subject and object. (*The Theory of the Novel*, 74–75)

Although Lukacs explains brilliantly how the intellectual male subject emerges dialectically from the sublation of the proletarian male subject, I want to call attention to the fact that he says nothing about how these subjects were constituted as *masculine* in the first place. Associating femininity with the detail and the internalized contradictions that, for him, lead to the ruin of the European novel, Lukacs is too concerned with negating femininity to be able to account for the gendered formation of the modern subject.

In *The Political Unconscious* (1981), Fredric Jameson, like Lukacs, reads the French realist novel as a dialectical genre. The realist novel identifies (or incorporates), critiques (or negates), and potentially overcomes (or sublates) the fragmentation of the male citizen-subject in capitalist society.[4] Unlike Lukacs, however, Jameson acknowledges that, for Balzac, family life exemplifies the aesthetic and social instability of nineteenth-century culture:

Yet this representation of a historical dialectic is at one and the same time the locus of an essentially ideological reflection, or in our previous terminology, of the mediation on a conceptual antinomy. From this angle, the problem is one of the ideological category of "violence" and can perhaps best be conveyed in the following formulation: how is it conceivable for the family to generate a force explosive enough to wrest the fortune away from its other branch without itself being blown open and destroyed in the process? (172)

On the one hand, according to Jameson, Balzac uses the new bourgeois nuclear family to displace the older alliance-based family of aristocratic culture. At the same time, Balzac represents the aristocratic family in a nostalgic manner that apparently undermines the legitimacy of the emergent bourgeois family. Having played both models of the family off one another in this mutually negating fashion, Jameson asks, has Balzac not destroyed the very construct of the family?

Jameson answers his own question by maintaining that "When we understand that the family is here, according to the canonical logic of Balzac's conservatism, the figure of society, it will become evident that the 'political unconscious' of this text is thereby raising, in symbolic form, issues of social change and counterrevolution, and asking itself how the force necessary to bring about a return to the old order can be imagined as doing so without at the same time being so powerful and disruptive as to destroy that order itself in the process" (173). By implicitly assuming that women embody the antithesis or negative properties of male citizens in both aristocratic and bourgeois cultures, Jameson cannot possibly explain why the family persists so stubbornly despite Balzac's mutually contradictory descriptions of it. A more nuanced literary reading of family relations in Balzac would reveal the important role played by women in ensuring the affective and moral stability of the family in the face of unsettling historical change. Such a reading, I plan to show, must follow the double dialectical logic of Balzac's representation of gender and, even more specifically, of the civic roles played by women and men in the modern nation-state.

Balzac is the optimal literary figure for a study of the expanding nineteenth-century French democracy. More than any other writer of his time, he depicts, in a series of novels grouped together under the name *Scènes de la Vie Privée,* the gendered division of spheres. Initially excluded from the public sphere, women were relegated to a private area associated with their supposedly natural domestic capabilities. This exclusion of women from the public sphere deprived them of citizenship status. Eventually, however, feminists and other social groups emphasized the civic importance of women's domestic responsibilities, arguing for their inclusion in the public sphere as citizen-subjects who are both like and unlike men. In *La Cousine Bette,* Balzac attempts to strengthen women's civic roles in the private sphere while also weakening their civic intervention in the "masculine" public sphere. In so doing, the author asserts that women should embody a different kind of citizen-subject status than men.

To accomplish this double objective, he follows a chiasmic process of gendering. This process places the androgynous woman outside of dialectically defined versions of both femininity and masculinity. As we recall, a double dialectics describes the semantic logic by which the identity of each sex is formed. It employs a process of negation, or the specification of what something is not. What men are not is generally associated with the concept of "women" (or nonmen) and, conversely, what women are not is generally associated with the concept of "men" (or nonwomen). By contrast to the Hegelian single dialectic, which begins only with a masculine subject and defines woman as its negative or opposite, a double dialectics takes both sexes as points of departure and through a process of reciprocal negation arrives at definitions of the citizen-subject.

What can be gained from analyzing Balzac's representation of the role played by the family in the emerging democracy in terms of the dynamics of the chiasmus? I believe that such an analysis can elucidate the cultural logic of the debates as to whether citizenship will be masculine or ambisexual, as well as explore the nature of women's and men's participation in citizenship. Looking at the formation of gender as a double dialectics enables us to see how women were positioned both inside and outside of the political economy of citizenship. Then as now, the issue of gender subordination is not as simple as it seems. There are compensations and inducements that accompany women's exclusion from the public sphere. In describing Balzac's double dialectical model of citizenship, I will also identify its internal contradictions. Balzac's text addresses the following questions: What happens when the double dialectical division of spheres between men and women fails; when women become involved in the masculine public sphere? What happens, for example, when courtesans like Josépha and Valérie or single women like Cousine Bette are compelled by market forces and personal circumstances to make their living in the masculine public sphere?[5] How does their negative sexual positioning—as neither feminine nor masculine citizen-subjects—affect the double dialectical economy of gendered citizenship outlined by Balzac's work?

According to *La Cousine Bette,* once women participate in the public sphere, they become androgynous, or uncategorizable in terms of traditional gender roles. Balzac's description of androgyny resembles my own. Rather than viewing androgyny as a harmonious synthesis of the sexes, he describes it as a selective incorporation and negation of both sexes or, in Hegelian terms, as a sublation of sexual difference. Once he sets up binary gender roles as desirable, Balzac depicts androgyny as a profoundly unsettling, even if fascinating, category of gender. The main question raised by this novel then becomes, how do those excluded from the new nuclear family unsettle its boundaries and destroy the gender norms that it establishes? To answer this question, let us turn to an analysis of *La Cousine Bette.*

THE BOURGEOIS MOTHER–WIFE:
THE NEW DOMESTIC CITIZEN-SUBJECT

In the beginning of the novel, the narrator simultaneously signals the wife's moral value and her husband's immorality by means of symbolic descriptions of their faded, though still valuable, furniture, which includes silk curtains, once red, but now faded to violet by the sun and frayed along the folds by long use, a carpet from which the colors had disappeared, chairs with their gilding rubbed off and their silk spotted with stains and worn threadbare in patches . . . (84)

The timeworn furniture symbolizes the neglect of the wife by her husband, who eventually sells even these faded relics of his once exclusive marital love to furnish the apartments of his mistresses. Already we observe a twofold dialectical process of gendering. Mme Hulot's virtue is given a position of prominence on the cultural stage and contrasted both with her husband's moral weakness (because he squanders their capital on other women) and with the lack of feminine virtue of the courtesan. The description of the furniture accentuates this contrast. We are led to believe that the courtesan's new furniture, obtained by means of her sexual services to rich men, cannot match Mme Hulot's dated but tasteful decor. Josépha's room may be stunning, full of "the gilding, the costly carving in the style known as Pompadour, the sumptuous materials—for any tradesman might have ordered and obtained these by the mere expenditure of an ocean of gold," but all this purchased luxury is excessive (84). It represents an attempt to simulate an older model of luxury without reproducing its class connotations. The new bourgeois furniture obtained by the courtesan thus cannot compare with Mme Hulot's inherited possessions. The simulacrum of luxury may outdo its aristocratic model, but its very excessiveness points to the limits of its imitation. Every object in Mme Hulot's apartment is as well chosen as the clothes she wears. The figures of the home and the wife represent a valorized feminine virtue essential to the civic order that nevertheless requires revitalization. The mother–wife becomes, for Balzac, both the object and agent of social reform.

When introducing us to the central figure of the bourgeois wife, the narrator focuses upon her incorruptible fidelity, virtue, and maternalism: "From the first days of her marriage until that moment, the Baroness had loved her husband . . . with an admiring love, a maternal love, with abject devotion . . . To reward her for this angelic kindness, she had gained her husband's veneration, and was worshipped by him as a kind of divinity" (31). The text states that M. Hulot reveres his wife and compares her to "our mother Eve." The novel, however, will not allow the wife to become in any way secondary to the husband, presumably Adam. On the contrary, Balzac informs us that young Baron Hulot is "as a man a replica of Adeline as a woman" (53). He therefore implies that woman is the primary subject and model of creation (in biblical terms) and of civic citizenship (in social terms).[6] The husband is depicted only negatively, as the repository of those civic qualities excluded from the definitions of the mother–wife, epitomized by Mme Hulot.

Thus, Balzac's text takes maternal and civic femininity as its initial point of departure for definitions of subject-citizenship. The novel begins by defining masculinity only in terms of femininity (as nonfemininity), not vice versa, as do androcentric definitions of the citizen-subject. The little we know about M. Hulot's behavior is (1) that he is nonvirtuous (which emphasizes, by contrast, his wife's virtue) and (2) that he worships his wife, which once again draws more attention to the qualities that make his wife worthy of veneration than to him. The reciprocal flow of marital affection depends upon the lasting moral and affective qualities of the wife. For what kind of wife deserves the constant worship of her husband? According to Balzac, only a wife of unwavering feminine virtue; one who sustains the disrupted stability of the family by the outside "public" world. The husband's part is not defined in relation to his affective and sexual exclusiveness—which he obviously lacks—but in relation to his continuing "worship" of his "angelic" wife. His duties as a spouse are thus conditioned upon his wife's ability to be a proper citizen-subject in her role as mother–wife since, as we remember, only in return for her "angelic kindness" did she gain "her husband's veneration, and was worshipped by him as a kind of divinity." Let me, however, not create the impression that the logic of the double dialectics is more advantageous to women in all respects than the older, single dialectical, model of gender formation. The conflation between women, domesticity, and virtue restricts women's behavior and leaves men with more freedom to act in the public sphere.

In fact, Balzac's text centralizes the mother–wife in the bourgeois household to compensate for the destabilizing mobility of her counterparts in the public sphere. Moreover, by valorizing the faithful wife who preserves the father's, and by extension the family's, public reputation, the novel does not succeed in establishing the domestic stability it seeks. Instead, it merely redefines familial stability not in terms of paternal virtue—as republican models of citizenship tend to do—but in terms of how well the virtuous mother can preserve the semblance of paternal responsibility. The narrator amplifies women's civic significance by depicting the welfare of the family as entirely dependent upon the wife's unwavering love, tolerance, and discretion. These qualities must be reflected in the beautiful and angelic signs of Mme Hulot's conformity to prevalent codes of femininity:

> She belonged to the company of perfect, dazzling beauties . . . whom Nature fashions with peculiar care, bestowing on them her most precious gifts: distinction, dignity, grace, refinement . . . Adeline Fisher, one of the most beautiful of this divine race, possessed the noble features, the curving lines, the veined flesh, of women born to be queens. (32)

The narrator empowers the wife within the domestic and civic spheres by means of (at least) three interrelated discourses: the natural, the social, and the moral.

First and foremost, Adeline embodies a perfect, dazzling masterpiece of "Nature" in contrast to the bestial appearance of the androgynous Cousine Bette. Adeline's "nature," however, shows no signs of animality. It is characterized as feminine and thus as fit to anchor the domestic and civic spheres only insofar as it excludes the sexuality and desire for power that define the masculinity of M. Hulot, Crevel, and Wencelas. Adeline's natural feminine beauty must be worked on, elaborated, and transformed by the simultaneously aesthetic and moral codes that exhibit the wife's "distinction, nobility, grace, refinement and elegance." Second, the wife's social graces ultimately elevate her to the level of the stately, as Adeline's natural distinction destines her to the "noble race . . . of women born to be queens." Once again, the wife's regal qualities are social. Being part of the declining aristocracy, Adeline is an asset to her nouveau-riche husband. Third, the narrator adds specific, more contextual qualifications that correlate the woman's moral strength to her class position:

> She would very much have liked the Baron to confide in her; but she had never dared to let him know that she knew of his escapades, out of respect for him. Such excessive delicacy is found only in girls of noble character sprung from the people, who know how to take blows without returning them. In their veins flows the blood of the early martyrs. (35)

In order to transform nobility of rank into nobility of character, Balzac replaces Mme Hulot's social nobility with a nobility of spirit. Although she is aristocratic by birth in contrast both to her *parvenu* husband and to the "androgynous" courtesans and governesses who elevate themselves by taking money, she is an impoverished aristocrat. Her ambivalent class position explains her natural and cultural "nobility"—her advantage over her husband—and her dependency upon him for money and access to Parisian high society. This economic and social debt is repaid not only by her cultural capital as an aristocrat, but also by her specifically feminine currency, virtue.

While the nobility of women can be, to use Lévi-Strauss's formulation, exchanged among men to consolidate patrilineal alliances, the "priceless" virtue of the new women is not subject to exchanges among men. Or at least, women play central roles as the subjects determining the nature of the exchanges, not only as the objects exchanged. When Crevel, a wealthy *parfumier*, tries to persuade Mme Hulot to betray her husband because he cheated on her, she refuses. She knows that the real reason Crevel wants her is, as he explicitly states, because "you are my vengeance" (40). Since

M. Hulot took his mistress, he decides that it is only fair "to take his wife. It's justice" (41). Mme Hulot refuses to regard her virtue as a commodity and responds only by "fixing this calculating bourgeois with a look of terror" (42). Rather than viewing herself as an object of sexual exchange—as does Crevel—Mme Hulot transforms feminine virtue as a gift that any respectable woman can make to her husband.

The concept of civic virtue, as delineated by the Napoleonic Code as well as by Balzac's novel, is thus gender-coded. A virtuous wife must remain loyal, obedient, and faithful to her husband so long as he does not completely destroy the family honor by squandering money on other women. The wife can never betray her husband since that would unsettle the patrilineal rights that establish masculine versions of citizenship. As the narrator advises, she must know how to "receive blows without returning them." The wife's social role is never to punish her husband. Instead, she must nudge and coax him into being the right (modern) kind of husband. Without voicing a word of reproach even when she knows that her husband neglects her and spends their money on courtesans, Mme Hulot continues to treat "her Hector like a mother treats her child" (52).

THE BOURGEOIS FATHER–HUSBAND:
THE NEW PUBLIC CITIZEN-SUBJECT

So far, Balzac's novel has positioned the mother–wife as both superior and inferior to the father–husband. On the one hand, if the wife did not have moral and affective superiority, the husband would not listen to her gentle discipline. On the other hand, unless she is economically disadvantaged, the wife will not be likely to possess the necessary humility to treat her husband's affairs leniently:

> Well-born girls, as their husband's equals, feel a need to bait their husbands, . . . to make up for their acts of tolerance by biting remarks, in a spirit of revengeful spite and in order to assure themselves of their own superiority or of their right to have their revenge. (53)

At this point, we begin to see the necessity of producing a masculine subject who is primarily, not only derivatively, a citizen-subject. In the second loop of the chiasmus, M. Hulot's social assets—namely, his title as a baron and his important military roles under the reign of Napoleon I and Louis-Philippe—are taken as the point of departure for definitions of citizenship. By contrast, the feminine subject becomes his negation, or excluded exterior:

For Adeline, the Baron was therefore from the beginning a kind of god who could do no wrong. She owed everything to him: fortune—she had her carriage, a fine house, all the luxury of the period; happiness, for she was openly loved; a title—she was a Baroness; celebrity—she was known as the beautiful Mme Hulot, and in Paris! (33–34)

In the male-centered loop of the chiasmus, Mme Hulot is defined by her husband's economic and social role, just as he has been defined in terms of her virtue in the first, female-centered, loop. The implication is that the wife may be superior to the husband in virtue and the fulfillment of domestic duties, but he is the primary citizen-subject and her anchor in the economic and political spheres. The wife's economic and political dependency upon the husband will not allow the process of gender formation to become a single dialectic centered upon the figure of the mother–wife. The interdependency between husband and wife transforms gender into a mutually defining relationship between masculine and feminine citizen-subjects.

The narrator cautions, however, that not all impoverished women are born with the ennobling qualities of the bourgeois wife. Starting from the same social position—namely, poverty—women can remain feminine by marrying relatively wealthy men or, like Cousine Bette and Valérie Marneffe, enter the masculine public sphere to make their own living. The contrast between merely female and feminine women establishes the mother–wife as the primary subject of civic virtue. The kinds of women who are biologically female but too culturally undomesticated to be properly feminine are represented as androgynous. Such women are neither feminine nor masculine; they are excluded from both domestic and public spheres. The cultural identity of androgynous women is therefore established by means of a sublation (or partial incorporation and partial negation) of masculine and feminine qualities.

On the one hand, such women are defined (along with men) as everything but virtuous, domestic, and tolerant: in other words, as the negation of the bourgeois mother–wife. On the other hand, androgynous women are also defined (along with feminine women) as the negation of the masculine citizen-subject. Unlike men, they do not have the right to direct political representation and tend to hold subordinate positions in the world of work. Both sharing and subverting gender roles, androgynous women are socially uncategorizable. Why would the very existence of androgynous women, established by a process of the double negation of sexual difference, threaten the division of spheres? I would like to propose that such women conceptually displace both masculinity and femininity by internalizing the double dialectics of gender formation. Let me explain.

The logic of the chiasmus assumes that sexual difference can be established by the mutual negations between a feminine and a masculine subject. Androgyny, as represented by women like Valérie and Cousine Bette, does not merely synthesize or combine masculine and feminine characteristics. It actually undermines the contradictions (or reciprocal negations) that define masculine and feminine citizen-subjects. On the one hand, androgynous women are described as subjects who, like men and contrary to feminine women, make their living in the public sphere. On the other hand, they are described as subjects who, like women and contrary to men, do not have political power. By chiasmically crossing the civic qualities that define both genders, androgynous women incorporate and displace gender-based traits in a way that eliminates the contradictions between the sexes. That is, they represent public life and feminine identity as a plausible combination, thus undermining the paradigm of femininity established by women's exclusion from the public sphere. Since, as I have demonstrated, Balzac's fiction proposes an oppositional model of sexual difference, we have every reason to expect that the existence of androgynous women will pose a threat to its cultural logic that the novel must eliminate at all cost. This is precisely what the last section of the novel attempts to achieve.

THE ANDROGYNOUS WOMAN: DISPLACING BOTH MASCULINE AND FEMININE MODELS OF SUBJECT-CITIZENSHIP

To criticize the effect of androgynous women on society, Balzac establishes a series of hierarchical contrasts between such improperly gendered women and the figure of the mother–wife. Courtesans such as Valérie and masculine spinsters such as Cousine Bette, Balzac suggests, constitute an entirely different breed. To impress readers with the negative qualities of such women, the narrator focuses upon the attributes that mark them as primitive rather than feminine:

> She held in check, only by her knowledge of law and the world, the primitive impetuous directness with which country people, like savages, translate emotion into action. In this directness, perhaps, lies the whole difference between primitive and civilized man. The civilized man has emotions plus ideas. (45)

In a civilized woman, understood as a woman who can stabilize the civic sphere, nature is always mediated by reflection. By way of contrast, Cousine Bette acts spontaneously, "like Savages." The dichotomy between nature and culture, or between savagery and civilization, is not constituted by means of a clear opposition so much as by their interdependency. Nature may dictate sentiments, but culture provides the tools to assess their appropriateness in any given circumstance. In light of this way of making distinctions, we can deduce that the danger posed by Cousine Bette consists not in her savagery alone, but in the fact that she regards culture as something to manipulate in the service of her desires.

The relations between "nature" and "culture" depicted in this passage initially follow a process of chiasmic inversion whereby Cousine Bette and Valérie represent the negation of Adeline as much as M. Hulot does. While Adeline's noble "nature" was from the beginning cultivated, the converse is true in Bette's and Valérie's cases. These androgynous women's "savage" natures seem to be thinly disguised beneath a surface layer of dissimulation. As the novel proceeds, however, it negates the dialectical opposition between civilized and savage women. If we accept such an opposition, implied by Balzac's statement that "The Savage has only feelings; civilized man has both sentiments and ideas," we realize that Cousine Bette is neither bestial nor civilized. She is motivated by personal jealousy and carefully plans how to acquire wealth and power to destroy her sexually differentiated opposites, the Hulots. Bette therefore combines both bestiality and cultural knowledge in a way that renders the very opposition of these terms confusing, if not completely meaningless.

Although he takes great pains to point out the danger posed by Bette's animality, Balzac also attempts to domesticate the savage in Bette by comparing her to a little monkey: "her strange clothes gave Cousin Bette such a bizarre appearance that at times she reminded one of the monkeys dressed up as women that children, in Savoy, lead about on a string" (45). Balzac's attempt to tame the "beast" in Bette, whose very name phonetically conflates "bestiality" with "stupidity," becomes transparent once the narrator compares her to a circus creature that even children can lead around on a leash. An unavoidable question arises: If she can be so easily ridiculed, then why does such a woman continue to pose an obstacle in the narrative's way of achieving its ultimate goal, namely, the formation of the nuclear family?

Women who participate as women in the masculine public sphere, Balzac suggests, question the naturalized basis on which the division of spheres depends. Thus, they raise the following questions: If women's bodies do not prevent them from earning a living or from interacting with men in the public sphere, then why should their bodies prevent them from voting, acquiring advanced education, entering the professions, or politically representing other individuals? Conversely, if being a woman did not necessarily imply that one had the sympathetic feelings necessary for influencing social policies, then maybe women's containment to the domestic sphere is not based on nature but on culture and the whims of men.

Finally, all this implies that maybe women and men are not by nature contraries, but instead exist in complementary relations that gain cultural currency to the degree that they appear to be only natural.

It is precisely this naturalization of sexual difference that Balzac's text offers with one hand and withdraws with the other. Much as the novel convinces readers that the Hulot couple are contradictory poles of a naturalized model of sexual difference, it also convinces us that Valérie and her husband, M. Marneffe, are identical poles of a new model of sexual identity. Valérie and Marneffe share the same goal—to get ahead socially in the Parisian world—and the same philosophy—to do it by using Valérie's body to manipulate rich men. Both husband and wife pose a threat to the nuclear family. Like Valérie, "This meagre little man, with wispy hair and beard . . . was exactly the type of man brought before the police courts on a charge of indecent offences" (64). The text emphasizes that Valérie and her husband differ from one another only in physical appearance, not in motivation and behavior. Rather than being opposites, they are the same, in opposition to the codes of sexual difference that they displace. The androgynous subject thus exposes the limits of the ostensibly natural social unit, based upon a division of labor between men and women.

The existence of androgynous women disturbs the logic of binary gender roles, in part because these women cannot be disciplined into becoming feminine subjects. Bette's masculinity is apparent even in a cursory glance: "A peasant girl from the Vosges, with everything that that implies: thin, dark, with glossy black hair, heavy eyebrows meeting across the nose in a tuft, long and powerful arms, and broad solid feet . . . there is a quick sketch of the spinster" (39). Just as she confuses the boundaries between masculinity and femininity and between public, private, and social domains, Bette displaces the boundaries of the nuclear family. Bette is both outsider and insider to the bourgeois familial and social structure. Clearly, her masculine appearance carries implications that are more than skin-deep. It implies an independence from men, a self-sufficiency, and an inflexible determination that problematize the feminine civic identity established by the figure of Mme Hulot. It is no accident that Bette had refused four marriage proposals: not so much because she disliked the men, but because she preferred to maintain her independent, mobile way of life: "Lisbeth was, indeed, very apprehensive of possible restriction of her liberty" (41). In part by choice, in part by necessity, cousine Bette belongs to a growing percentage of single women in nineteenth-century France (and England) with ambiguous social status. Like most of Balzac's characters, Bette represents not only an individual but a social type. She epitomizes the androgynous spinster who cannot be integrated into the bourgeois family, yet who at the same time is an economic by-product of bourgeois society.

Because she works for a living and does not depend on a man for her economic subsistence and legal status, the single woman is considered more like a man than a woman. On this basis, some political thinkers argued that single and working women should be granted the same citizenship rights as men. Other, more reactionary social theorists regarded single and working women as a social and moral danger and proposed strategies to feminize single women.[7] Both sides could not avoid facing the economic necessity that some women, especially those who did not marry, had to work for a living.[8] For this reason, many women in fact became culturally androgynous, in the sense that they transformed the division of spheres maintained by the bourgeois model of the family.

Because she remains free and unattached, Bette can penetrate almost any domain—that of the wife and of the mistress, the private and public—circulating and negotiating, duplicitously or not, between them. Although by associating her strength with "virginity" the narrator hints that Bette does not have a comparable sexual freedom to the men in this novel, she far exceeds their social mobility and individual power. This is how the narrator justifies this woman's extraordinary strength:

> Virginity, like all abnormal states, has its characteristic qualities, its fascinating greatness. Life, whose forces have been kept unspent, takes on in the virgin individual an incalculable power of resistance and endurance. The brain has been enriched by the sum of all of its untapped faculties. (118)

Not without some degree of admiration, the narrator views Bette's prolonged virginity—and perhaps even the "untapped faculties" that get channeled into her strength, independence, and tenacity—as nonfeminine and even "monstrous" qualities that constitute Bette's "fascinating greatness."[9] It is not accidental that this text presents feminine potency as resulting from sexual latency. The implication is: Had Bette married like a proper woman should, she would have lost the physical and psychological qualities of a man and become acceptably domestic. The novel thus suggests that the qualities generally considered to be masculine and feminine are not naturally present. They are tendencies that must be cultivated as one conforms to civic practices, either within or outside of the nuclear family. Without the family structure functioning as a foundation for other social relations, both men and women risk becoming socially uncategorizable, subversive, and androgynous.

Much as conservatives predicted an inversion of power relations once women were "masculinized" by their participation in politics,[10] so Balzac argues that Bette's masculinity inverts such relations in her behavior toward her adopted son, Wencelas: "L'amour de la domination resté dans ce coeur de vieille fille, à l'état de germe, se développa rapidement. Elle put satisfaire son orgueil et son besoin d'action: n'avait-elle pas une créature à elle, à gronder, à diriger, à flatter, à rendre heureuse, sans avoir à craindre aucune rivalité?" (96). After being chiasmically contrasted with the figure of the wife, Bette displaces the figure of the husband by assuming the authoritative role of the father in her relationship with her adopted son.

Let us reflect on what happens as the figure of the androgynous woman passes through the two loops of the chiasmus. The first loop identifies the mother–wife (feminine subject A) as its point of departure and defines both the father–husband (masculine subject B) and the androgynous woman as its negation. The second loop takes the father–husband (masculine subject B') and the androgynous woman as its point of departure and defines the mother–wife as their negation (feminine subject A'). Thus, when Bette uses the term *rival*, it applies equally well to a potential father-figure as to a wife. Bette fulfills both civic functions in her inclusive role as parent and virgin. She manages to preserve her all-encompassing familial relationship to Wencelas not only by maintaining his dependency upon her financial resources and emotional support, but also by restricting his mobility. In other words, she behaves like a nineteenth-century father would with his dependent daughter or wife. Thus, when the young man attempts to make Bette aware of his sexual desire, which ordinarily would be considered a male privilege, she denies him this right by arguing:

> You want to ruin your health in the stews of Paris, and end up like so many artists, dying in the workhouse! No, no make a fortune for yourself first, and when you have money stacked away you can take your fun then, my child. You will have the wherewithal then, you libertine, to pay the doctors as well as the pleasures! (70)

Once again, Bette differentiates herself from the bourgeois wife and the bourgeois husband, while dialectically incorporating the cultural functions and definitions of both. On the one hand, she behaves as a father would with his daughter. On the other hand, Bette fulfills the feminine function of restraining male sexual desire, as a virtuous wife and mother should. Rather than operating within the ideal wife's sympathetic ethical framework, however, this disciplinary woman produces pragmatic arguments capable of dominating men. Bette's authority over Wencelas depends upon "a bizarre alliance . . . of a powerful will acting incessantly on a weak character," as well as upon a gender-role reversal such that one "might have thought that Nature had made a mistake in assigning their sexes"

(87). Thus, Bette's androgynous self-sufficiency does not merely decenter the role of the father (as does Mme Hulot's feminine virtue), but it also effectively displaces the father. The husband–father—or the male citizen-subject—has no place in the type of family ambisexually ruled by Bette.

Having assumed and displaced the role of the father, she does the same for the role of the mother. In fact, Bette poses a threat to the new bourgeois family not only because she confuses masculine and feminine functions, but also because she creates tensions for more conventional characters. One of the most effective means by which she infiltrates the Hulot family—in order to destroy it from within—consists of her penetration of its "private" nuclear boundaries by making herself indispensable to the Hulot women:

> Her absolute discretion earned her the trust of elder people too, for, like Ninon, she had some masculine qualities . . . Everyone believed this poor spinster to be so dependent that she had no alternative but to keep her mouth shut. Cousin Bette herself called herself the family confessional. Only the Baroness felt . . . some mistrust. (45)

This passage draws the boundaries of "the private" very close to the center of the family by restricting it solely to the husband and wife. It is interesting, and even surprising, that Bette's discretion is deemed "masculine" while that of Mme Hulot's displays exemplary femininity. By such contradictions, the novel compels us to ask when feminine dissimulation is considered a source of social corruption and when is it considered a proper bourgeois wife's duty? As we have seen in the analysis of Valérie and Bette's deceitful behavior—which is contrasted to Mme Hulot's dutiful façade—the criteria between legitimate and illegitimate feminine deception are not all that easy to distinguish.

The notion of dissimulation itself has a long cultural history that is important to the consolidation of subject-citizenship in France. Lynn Hunt demonstrates that during and immediately following the French Revolution, dissimulation was regarded as a threat to the new democratic society. Too easily assimilated to aristocratic practices, where the visible signs of class were manipulated for political purposes, republican discourses privileged transparency, or the undistorted expression of the private self in the public sphere.[11] Without clearly subverting this cultural model, Balzac nuances it by articulating the standards that distinguish right and wrong kinds of feminine dissimulation.

In *La Cousine Bette,* the concept of dissimulation lies at the core of cultural strategies to consolidate a stable bourgeois family without curtailing masculine freedom. According to this novel, some aspects of the new femininity—particularly the kind exercised by public women—certainly should be considered dangerous, especially for men. But other kinds of feminine dissimulation, including the secrecy between husband and wife, preserve the social order. Consequently, using physical appearance and dissimulation as an instrument of power is both encouraged and distrusted. While being defined as a seductive, beautiful surface, women are at the same time not supposed to use their physical beauty to deceive or corrupt men, except, of course, when masculine codes call for such deception. As Balzac's fiction illustrates, however, as feminine dissimulation becomes both necessary and dangerous for the social order, its effects become increasingly difficult to predict and control.

To be constructive, feminine dissimulation must observe clear boundaries between the private and public domains: between harmful information that must remain a secret between husband and wife, and harmless information that can be shared with others. Neither the children nor most of the elder family members can be trusted with potentially destabilizing secrets. Kinship relations are presented as unreliable. It is only nuclear ties, and more specifically the chiasmic relations between husband and wife, the novel suggests, that can be trusted. There is a good conceptual and cultural reason for this rejection of kinship relations. Historically, kinship relations have not defined the existence of masculine and feminine subjects in terms of each other. Although the nature of kinship is too complicated for me to be able to describe it here, I can state that kinship relations are generally produced by a single dialectical process (they are patrilineal or, more rarely, matrilineal). Furthermore, kinship relations are concerned primarily with the consolidation of alliances and the distribution of capital rather than with the formation of gendered citizen-subjects.[12]

Bette represents this older model of the family. Her primary motivation for wishing to destroy her cousin's life is that, not being beautiful like Adeline, she lacks the "feminine capital" to make a good match, escape poverty, and establish her own family. Failing to fulfill the model of the new domestic woman, she falls back upon an older model of kinship relations. Accordingly, she moves in with her cousin's family and attempts to manipulate them in such a way as to appropriate their wealth. In so doing, Bette not only represents an alarming model of the future "androgynous" subject, but also reasserts kinship relations before the new nuclear family has been consolidated. The nuclear family depends upon a replacement of alliance-based ties, represented by women like Bette, with affective ties, maintained by women like Adeline.

For a long time Mme Hulot was able to preserve the stability and well-being of her family by keeping her husband's extramarital affairs secret not only from her children, but also from the rest of the family. Praising

Mme Hulot's "feminine" discretion, the narrator informs us that this exemplary wife shares her secrets only with God. Once these private secrets come to be known and circulated in the public sphere, however, the boundaries of the nuclear family begin to disintegrate. The fact that the Hulot children habitually confide in Cousine Bette, an extended member of the family who shares "private" secrets with outsiders like Valérie, confuses the boundaries between private and public spheres.

Balzac's narrative uses a three-step process to redefine bourgeois society. First, it contracts the boundaries of the private sphere to the nuclear family and especially to the conjugal couple. At the same time, by depicting the strengths and potentially positive influence of the bourgeois wife, the novel widens the boundaries of the private sphere to intersect with the expanding feminized social sphere. Finally, by defining the public sphere as the masculine realm excluded from the feminized "private" and "social" spheres, the text once again distinguishes masculine from feminine citizen-subjects. At some point or another, however, all of these distinctions are subverted by the intervention of androgynous women who blur the boundaries between private and public domains.

By describing, if only ironically, M. Hulot's disastrous experience with Valérie, the bourgeois courtesan, the narrator sensitizes readers to the danger of androgynous women:

> For, certainly, in her there was no sight of the derision, the debauchery, the wild extravagance, the moral depravity, the contempt for social properties, the complete independence, which, in the actress and the singer, had been the cause of his sufferings. (107–108)

Balzac's novel presents the bourgeois courtesan as far more pernicious to the family than the old type of aristocratic courtesan. The threat posed by Valérie is similar to the one posed by her accomplice, Bette. Both women are able to pose as virtuous and kind (i.e., as conventional women) when they are actually morally versatile and opportunistic (which is how conventional men are described by the novel). Furthermore, whereas the need for sexual conquest is depicted as a natural masculine quality, it appears it could just as well be feminine. We find out, for instance, that "Valérie had admirably appropriated for herself the baron Hulot" (178). Similarly, Bette speaks with relish of procuring herself a man (as if he were a household pet), explaining, "You see, I have neither cat . . . nor dog, nor parrot; it makes sense for an old maid like myself to have some little thing to love, to torment; so . . . I got myself a Pole" (69). Once again, such women's selective incorporation and negation of both masculine and feminine identities challenge gender oppositions. The narrator cautions us that

"These Machiavellis in skirts are the most dangerous women" (173). Indeed, even the ostensible referent—namely, woman's material body—cannot be trusted as a sign of femininity in androgynous women.

Valérie's Machiavellian politics include such strategies as:

> When the world was present she displayed an enchanting combination of dreamy, modest innocence, impeccable propriety, and native wit, enhanced by charm, grace, and easy Creole manners. But in private conversation she outdid the courtesans, she was droll, amusing, fertile in invention. (161)

The bourgeois courtesan's greatest skill consists of knowing how to manipulate the feelings and desires of relatively wealthy men. Unlike aristocratic courtesans, who could be identified as such by their public performances as opera singers, actresses, or dancers, Balzac's bourgeois courtesan can hide her true vocation behind her wedding veil and social status. She is consequently difficult to contain and regulate for the public use of men. Women like her move from the public to the private sphere, threatening the autonomy of private life: "Thanks to these romantic, sentimental, novelettish maneuvers, Valérie, without having promised anything, obtained for her husband the position of deputy head clerk of his office and the Cross of the Legion of Honor" (105). Valérie's duplicitous role, as middle-class wife and public courtesan, enables her to change her behavior to meet the fantasies of modern men.

Mme Hulot has no such capability. She regards her public duties as an extension of her private role as the educator of the family, while her husband cavorts with prostitutes in public. The courtesan confuses gender difference because she conforms neither to masculine nor to feminine norms of sexual behavior. In private she behaves much as the bourgeois husband does in public and so becomes the negation of femininity. In public, however, she behaves like the bourgeois wife does in private and so becomes the negation of masculinity. The effect of this narrative logic is gender chaos because, as I have argued so far, it has eliminated the naturalized opposition between the sexes. Balzac's fear is that if a single subject embodies the gender processes that should be produced by the chiasmic relations between two such subjects, gender itself and the division of spheres are rendered obsolete. What does Balzac do to prevent such a disastrous outcome?

As a precaution against the temptation posed by economically ambitious women such as Valérie, the text modifies the ideal of the virtuous wife. It tries to do so by attempting to incorporate within marriage the sexual fantasies provoked and satisfied by the courtesan. With some humor, the narrator states that the new ideal wife should adhere to the following precept:

To be a virtuous and even prudish woman in the world's eyes, and a courtesan to her husband, is to be a woman of genius . . . In such genius lies the secret of these long attachments that are inexplicable to women without the gift of such paradoxical yet superb abilities. (199)

Unfortunately, the strategy of having the feminine citizen-subject behave in a manner considered masculine only amplifies gender confusion since it undermines the paradigm of domestic femininity valorized by the novel. As we have seen, the narrative logic of the text itself destroys the ideal of the mother–wife not only thematically, but also structurally. Since the courtesan can play the role of the virtuous wife in public, this logic implies, the wife can save the family only by playing the role of the courtesan in private. By becoming a courtesan to her husband, the wife can reduce the dangerous temptation posed by real courtesans. At the beginning of the novel Mme Hulot functioned as the normative standard by which the identities of men and of androgynous women were constituted through a dialectical process of negation. By the end of the novel, however, it is the androgynous woman who constitutes that norm. Women like Mme Hulot are required to imitate the courtesan. Once praised, Mme Hulot's virtuous behavior appears exaggerated and naive:

The look with which the baron rewarded the fanaticism of his wife confirmed her opinion that sweetness and submission were women's most powerful weapons. She was wrong. Noble sentiments pushed to an extreme produce the same results as the greatest vices. (p. 201)

The positive social effects of virtuous women begin to resemble the negative effects of androgynous women. The very distinction between civic virtue and perversion is confused along with the distinction between women and men. Women are no longer being asked to be feminized by being selfless, virtuous, coy, or gentle in exercising moral discipline upon their husbands and children. Instead, they are encouraged to be the opposite of feminine—in other words, strategic, duplicitous, and self-serving. A novel that began by proposing a model of sexual difference ended up endorsing gender confusion.

Evidently aware of this problem, Balzac attempts a spectacular solution to gender and moral chaos by eliminating the androgynous woman. Adopting much the same strategy as he did when calling Bette a "savage" and "monkey," Balzac reduces Valérie's allure by unpeeling her layers of artifice to expose the essential beast:

She had the cool indifference of cats, who run and pounce only when obliged to by necessity. She required life to be all pleasure, and pleasure to be all calm plain sailing ... These courtesan tastes Valérie derived from her mother. (117)

Nature and culture appear to be inseparable in this description, as Valérie's love of luxury is described as feline. Two interrelated issues need to be raised concerning this passage. First, why does Balzac present Valérie's essential being as natural when he has taken such pains to describe it in terms of the theatrical roles she plays? Second, why does he then proceed to partly reintegrate this natural insolence into the realm of culture, by attributing it to a maternal influence? I would propose that Balzac's narrative strategy focuses upon two central modes of domesticating the androgyne. The first consists of downplaying the threat she embodies through his choice of metaphors. By describing Bette as a monkey rather than a savage, and Valérie as an indolent cat rather than a predatory tigress, he symbolically reduces the power of a force that evidently cannot find a satisfactory resolution within the social categories of his time. He further civilizes the intimidating animal nature of these exceptional women by explaining the cultural factors that have created them. In Valérie's case, the text holds maternal education directly responsible for either humanizing or animalizing the child. This strategy offers the author yet another opportunity to emphasize the civic significance of the virtuous mother–wife.

In fact, the greatest danger posed by Valérie consists not of her ability to tempt the husband away from his wife, but of her ability to strike directly at the unsuspecting virtuous wife herself: "This sketch gives innocent souls some faint idea of the various havocs that the Madame Marneffes of this world may wreak in families, and by what means they can strike at poor virtuous wives, apparently so far beyond their reach" (272). Deviation from gender norms might well be contagious. The text describes any such deviation as a slippery slope that initially establishes, but eventually obliterates, the dichotomies between proper and improper women. Exceptional women like Valérie attract men away from their conventional wives, thus destroying the nuclear family. In addition, such women demonstrate that masculine behavior can be advantageous to women. They show that conventional gender roles can restrict women, even as they claim to enhance their civic power. Thus, after idealizing the figure of the mother–wife and criticizing both the androgyne and the husband, Balzac's novel suggests that the mother–wife must resemble the courtesan in order to prevent the naturally desirous husband from destroying the family.

To deal with the logical corner into which he has painted himself, Balzac eliminates the characters of Valérie and her accomplice husband by having them contract a rare African venereal disease. Not without a certain punitive relish,[13] he mentions that "That poor woman, who was pretty so I am told, is well punished for now if she was proud of her beauty, for she's hideously ugly. . . . Her teeth and hair are falling out; she looks like a leper; she's an object of horror to herself" (420). Significantly, the narrator adds that this illness is characteristic of "blacks and native americans, whose immune systems differ from those of the white races" (420). Thus, we are to assume the biological superiority of "white races" over the "native peoples," in this way linking Valérie's natural inferiority to the Otherness of a colonial subject.

But the relations between nature and culture and among masculinity, femininity, and androgyny played out by this text are much too complex to be resolved by this simple solution. By this I do not mean only that by eliminating these two androgynous women, Balzac has not eliminated the social problems created by other women like them. We can interpret these women as representative of their types and Balzac's elimination of them as a symptomatic gesture proposing the elimination of all androgynous women. More seriously, Balzac's narrative demonstrates why such women cannot be eliminated and why, therefore, the nuclear family and the civic order endorsed by the text must be modified to accept their existence.

Balzac outlines the ideal social configuration—based upon a chiasmic interrelation between male and female citizen-subjects—and shows not only why this cultural model is desirable, but also why it is doomed to failure. On the surface, it would seem that the bourgeois nuclear family is destroyed not from within, but from without, by economic conditions that force some women to behave like men: to work, remain single, move about freely in the public sphere, and have multiple sexual relations while still retaining the aura of bourgeois respectability. When women take on masculine civic attributes, they destabilize the division of spheres. Yet when we examine more closely Balzac's narrative, we discover that the problem is not so much the gender exception as the gender-based rule. Cousine Bette, Josépha, Valérie, and their kind operate as exceptions not to an ideal norm of femininity but to a flawed chiasmic economy of sexual difference.

This model can be called flawed from both a historical and a conceptual perspective. Historically, the virtuous mother–wife looms as more of a mythical construct than her androgynous counterpart. By this I mean that this model is a regulative ideal—a prescription that can only be approximated by "real" women. I also mean to suggest that the material conditions that contributed to the formation of the bourgeois nuclear family in turn determined that working-class women often had to work to supplement the salaries of their husbands (hence the term "supplemental wages," coined to depict women's wages). To the same historical pressure we can attribute an increasing market for courtesans and prostitutes within the developing capitalist metropolises. In other words, so-called androgynous women were as much a part of the double dialectics of gender as were the respected feminine women.

Furthermore, while arguing that the division of spheres is founded upon men's and women's contradictory natures, the novel also shows us how this division is culturally produced and how it can be undermined. Beginning by idealizing the bourgeois wife as the fulcrum of social order, Balzac's novel concludes by simultaneously criticizing and praising the androgynous woman as the standard of new femininity. Women are confronted with a double-bind: Either they stay within the domestic sphere as does Mme Hulot and end up losing power over their husbands, or they define themselves as inferior women and acquire power over men in the public sphere.

As Lukacs's and Jameson's works predict (regarding masculine subjects), this class distinction within the category of "women" causes a breakdown in the modern definition of the female citizen-subject. The different kinds of androgynous women in Balzac's novels illustrate that precisely because women occupy such different socioeconomic positions, their containment within the private and social spheres proves difficult, if not impossible. The legal and normative contradictions and debates regarding the sociopolitical status of aristocratic versus working-class women, of working women versus housewives, and of single versus married women were an inevitable effect of the overdetermination of women, who could not be reduced to prevalent middle-class definitions of womanhood.

Second, Balzac's depiction of the chiasmic relations between husband and wife is inherently flawed from the point of view of what it attempts to accomplish. Contrary to James McGuire's claim that Balzac regrets "the erosion of traditional social values based on heredity" and patriarchal power,[14] I have argued that Balzac endorses and contributes to this erosion by valorizing the figure of the new bourgeois woman. Yet his critique of the patriarch, as well as the creation of female characters who do not conform to the proposed feminine ideal, undermines his social objectives. Once the mother–wife assumes the civic role of moral guide of the family, the father is chiasmically defined as not having those qualities and responsibilities. But without those virtues, the figure of the father is morally weak and relatively defenseless against the ploys and domination of androgynous women.[15] Although the men depend upon the existence of subversive women sexually, and sometimes even financially, these women cause the downfall of patriarchal society by destroying the complementary balance between husbands and wives. They are the constitutive contradiction of a culture where women are represented as external to the masculine public sphere yet, due to economic and sexual necessities, are at the same time an integral part of that public sphere.

On the one hand, Balzac constructs a paradoxical gender paradigm, where men are depicted as too weak to assume conventional masculine roles—including political leadership in citizenship—but where women are not encouraged to assume them either. On the other hand, Balzac's figurations of a failed patriarchal order where the division of spheres breaks down leave space for feminist interventions. As Denise Riley and Joan Scott demonstrate, nineteenth-century feminists employed the contradictory positioning of women with respect to subject-citizenship to their advantage. Feminists claimed the civic importance of conventional women in their roles as mothers and social benefactors in the private and social spheres. At the same time, they also subverted the division of spheres by supporting the growing number of androgynous women who made their living, by necessity or desire, in the masculine public sphere. These two complementary yet paradoxical strategies, both of which are represented—without necessarily being endorsed—by Balzac's *La Cousine Bette,* indicate some of the ways in which sociopolitical power can be extended from a few exceptional cases of androgynous women to all women. Conversely, Balzac's novel also shows even more convincingly how the domestic power and social influence with which mother–wives are invested can be exercised by all women.

NOTES

1. In "The Law's Contradictions," in *A History of Women in the West: Emerging Feminism to World War*, Nicole Armand-Duc analyzes the Napoleonic Code's inequitable treatment of women as well as the self-contradictions it encounters in differentiating among classes of women—and granting them different legal rights—based upon their marital and financial status.

2. For a discussion of these sociopolitical debates, see Geneviève Fraisse's *Muse de la raison.*

3. Georg Lukacs, *The Theory of the Novel: A Historico-Philosophical Essay on the Forms of Great Epic Literature*, 60. See also Lukacs's discussion of realism in *The Historical Novel.*

4. See Frederic Jameson's *The Political Unconscious: Narrative as a Socially Symbolic Act.*

5. Nicole Mozet also raises the question of whether or not Balzac's depiction of la cousine Bette constitutes an empowering representation of women in her article "La Cousine Bette: Roman du pouvoir féminin?" in *Balzac et les parents pauvres*, 33–45. She concludes that Balzac represents working and assertive women more as a social nightmare than as a reality. What may have been a night-

mare for Balzac, however, became an increasingly accepted social reality during the nineteenth century.

6. For further demonstration of this argument, see James R. McGuire, "The Feminine Conspiracy in Balzac's *La Cousine Bette*," in *Nineteenth-Century French Studies*, 295–296.

7. As Elinor A. Accampo documents in "Gender, Social Policy, and the Third Republic," in *Gender and the Politics of Social Reform in France, 1870–1914*: "Large-scale industrialization, which had intensified during the 1850s and 1860s, in many areas restructured work for both women and men. . . . The proportion of French women in the labor force increased steadily from about 24 percent in 1850 to about 43 percent in 1920" (4). Women's work in the public sphere, however, was viewed as problematic. On the one hand, as Accampo et al. illustrate, it was viewed as a threat to the family and gender roles. On the other hand, it was re-garded as a social necessity. As Accampo argues, "Women could not simply be relegated to the private sphere because they already had a public presence and public function in the productive labor they performed outside the home. More-over, their reproductive functions assumed a new social importance. Concerns about womanhood coincided with the formation of the Republic and efforts to implement new conceptions of citizenship" (10). As we have seen, Balzac's fic-tion both reflects and in some ways anticipates these cultural debates.

8. In *La Raison des femmes*, Geneviève Fraisse argues that single and other "ex-ceptional" women were authorized, or at least much more so than bourgeois wives, to make their living in the masculine public sphere: "Likewise, a woman who had to earn her living, a spinster, a widow, could be excused for being a woman writer. In brief, all women without a protector or resources, [were] au-thorized to take on paid work . . . This distinction between unmarried and mar-ried women is fundamental to understanding the interplay between exclusion and inclusion: because the unmarried woman, even if she did not have all male civil rights, benefitted at least from the ones that placed the juridical system in contradiction with itself" (178, my translation).

9. In "La Science: Modèle ou vérité, réflexions sur l'avant-propos à *La Comédie humaine*," in *Balzac: L'Invention du roman*, Françoise Gaillard discusses the influ-ence of empirical science and transformational/evolutionary theories on Balzac's fiction, particularly the influence of Cuvier and Saint-Hilaire upon Balzac's com-parisons of social and animal life.

10. For a discussion of these debates, see Geneviève Fraisse's *La Raison des femmes* and Joan Scott's *Only Paradoxes to Offer*.

11. In *The Family Romance of the French Revolution*, Lynn Hunt argues, "It was the definition of virtue, and as such it was imagined to be critical to the future of the republic. Dissimulation, in contrast, threatened to undermine the repub-lic: it was the chief ingredient in every conspiracy; it lay at the heart of the coun-terrevolution. . . . Dissimulation was also described in the eighteenth century as a characteristic feminine quality, not just an aristocratic one. According to Montesquieu and Rousseau, it was [corrupt] women who taught men how to dissimulate, how to hide their true feelings in order to get what they wanted in the public arena. The salon was the most important site of this teaching. And it was also the one place where society women could enter the public sphere. In a

sense, then, women in public were (like prostitutes) synonymous with dissimulation, with the gap between public and private" (96–98).

12. See Nancy Armstrong's explanation of the implications of the transition from an alliance-based to a nuclear model of the family for definitions of subjectivity in *Desire and Domestic Fiction*. See also Thierry Bloss's and Alain Frieckey's historical analyses of the changes in family structure between the Middle Ages and the modern period. Between the Middle Ages and the eighteenth century, the authors claim, the family was communitarian and kinship-based. Parents and children lived with grandparents, aunts, uncles, cousins, and other family members. Moreover, in aristocratic families, family members often lived in the same house with their many servants as well. In such crowded quarters, nuclear family ties did not get a chance to develop. The industrial revolution, which revolutionized living conditions, as well as texts such as Balzac's, contributed to the development of the modern nuclear family.

13. For further analysis of Balzac's convenient solution to the problem of androgynous women, see again McGuire's "The Feminine Conspiracy in Balzac's *La Cousine Bette*." As McGuire points out, "There is something suspicious about the deaths of Lisbeth Fischer and Valérie Marneffe. Bette dies outside of the narrative, parenthetically, of a 'phtisie pulmonaire,' yet she is the title character; the scene of Valérie's death is rife with melodrama and moral symbolism. The awkward, expeditious elimination of these two principal female figures leads one to question the actual nature of their transgressive role in *La Cousine Bette*" (295).

14. McGuire, "The Feminine Conspiracy in Balzac's *La Cousine Bette*," 295.

15. In this case, I would agree with McGuire that "The . . . men in the novel are characterized as either doddering philanderers (Hulot), ostentatious bourgeois (Crevel), infantilized and feminized objects of feminine desire (Steinbock), or exceedingly uninteresting (Victorin)" (295).

4

Exemplary Androgyny
in Sand's *Indiana*

For more than a century critics have drawn parallels between, and sometimes even conflated, (auto)biographical details about Sand's life, her ideological positions, and idealist aesthetics to construct what could be called Sand's "multiple androgynies."[1] By alluding to Sand's "androgynies," I refer to the sum of the contradictory interpretations that describe Sand's life and fiction as either masculine, feminine, or a mixture of both gender characteristics. Infamous for dressing as a man and adopting a man's *nom de plume*, Sand was both praised and castigated as the epitome of the virile woman.[2] Her representations of gender relations have been read as implying both "masculine" and "feminine" positions on the part of the author. Focusing upon Sand's criticisms of the institution of marriage as a means of subordinating women to men, some critics label Sand's ideology as feminine or proto-feminist.[3] Focusing upon her repudiation of feminist goals, especially women's right to citizenship, other critics consider Sand's ideological stance as masculine and reactionary.[4]

Sand's fiction underwent an equally contradictory or androgynous process of gendering as her (auto)biographical persona and sociopolitical views. As Sand indicates in the autobiographical narrative *Histoire de ma vie*, critics used their knowledge of (or speculation about) her gender identity to attribute essential masculine or feminine properties to her fiction. Sand recounts that when critics initially assumed, on the basis of her pseudonym, that she was a male author, "All the newspapers talked of M. G. Sand with praise, insinuating that a woman's touch must have passed over here and there to reveal to the author certain delicacies of the heart and mind, but declaring that the style and the commentaries had

65

too much truth not to have been written by a man" (vol. II, 174, my translation). Clearly, critics have taken Sand's pseudonym as an index not only of the author's gender, but also of an essential masculine aesthetic that would justify their claim that the author was a man. These critics have further assumed that, at least according to the emerging realist aesthetics,[5] only a male author would be able to represent the world "truthfully" in fiction. By contrast, a female author—and, correlatively, her feminine style—could function only as a supplement to a normatively masculine creation that reveals to the author "certain delicacies of the heart and mind." Thus, while masculine style functions as the foundation for a truthful representation of life, feminine style only provides additional nuances.[6] We could say that realism's claim to truthfulness depends upon its ability to establish its difference from a supposedly nontruthful but sensitive feminine aesthetics.

As soon as critics discovered the sex of the author, as Sand explains, they began to find typically feminine weaknesses of style and to discover "immoral" tendencies in her fiction. Political topics that seemed appropriate for a male author—such as the institution of marriage and slavery—were deemed inappropriate for a female author (*Histoire de ma vie*, 182). It is evident that, depending upon their assumptions about the author's sex and interpretations of her style, critics have imposed different, and indeed contradictory, gender attributes to Sand's work. If analyzed in terms of the logic of interpretation they follow, however, it quickly becomes apparent that these readings support rather than contradict each other.

The interpretations of Sand's fiction as either masculine or feminine, I would argue, rely upon what I have called a single dialectical reading of the process of gendering. As we recall, in a single dialectic of gender, the male subject acquires its positive identity as it negates the features that designate femininity. If realism provides a truthful representation of the world, then, according to the logic of a single dialectic, a feminized aesthetics will offer a contrastingly distorted, or idealized, version of the real. It is the very untruthfulness of feminine idealism that helps establish, by contrast, the truthfulness and legitimacy of masculine aesthetics. Such a contrast distinguishes not only masculine realism from feminine idealism, but also masculine and feminine forms of idealism.

In his critique of Romanticism in the pamphlet *Les Femmelins* (1858), for example, Proudhon warns against the perversion of masculine aesthetics by feminine idealism: "Any progressive or if one prefers developing literature," Proudhon claims, "is characterized by the movement of the idea, the masculine element; any decadent literature can be readily identified by the clouding of the idea, which is replaced by an excessive loquacity, which emphasizes falsity of thought, the poverty of the moral style, and . . . the hollowness of the style" (27–28).[7] In contrasting two gendered

forms of idealism, Proudhon establishes the progressive and positive nature of masculine idealism by means of a single dialectical logic that negates feminine idealism. He associates feminine idealism with all the undesirable qualities that masculine idealism must reject in order to retain
its identity: including untruthfulness, superfluous detail, digression, and
immorality. In so doing, Proudhon validates the veracity, appropriateness,
and virtue of masculine style. His association of feminine idealism with
the inessential, superfluous detail is a common gesture of nineteenth-
century criticism, as Naomi Schor has famously observed:

> To focus on the detail and more particularly on the *detail as negativity* is to
> become aware that the normative aesthetics elaborated and disseminated by
> the Academy is not sexually neutral; it is an axiology carrying into the field
> of representation the sexual hierarchies of the phallocentric cultural order.
> The detail does not occupy a conceptual space beyond the laws of sexual
> difference: the detail is gendered and doubly gendered as feminine. (*Read-
> ing in Detail,* 4)

If a male author were to adopt what Proudhon calls a feminine style of
writing, such gender confusion would necessarily corrupt a masculine
idealism that depends upon the exclusion of so-called feminine stylistic
elements. Proudhon's logic thus depends upon two interrelated axioms:
first, a conflation between an author's sex and gender-based conventions
and, second, a clear differentiation and, indeed, opposition between essential (or masculine) and inessential (or feminine) literary properties.
When one turns to Sand's fiction, however, it soon becomes clear that her
works violate the neat gender boundaries and defy the logic that critics
such as Proudhon would impose upon them.

This essay will perform a symptomatic reading of the gender, class, and
race constructs encoded in Sand's first novel, *Indiana* (1832),[8] to propose
a possible answer to the following question: What has led critics to
conflate so obsessively and yet disagree so vehemently about the gender
codes governing Sand's life, sexual ideology, and art of fiction? In raising
this question, along with Schor, I begin from the assumption that it is not
enough to claim that Sand's work has been read and described in gender-
based terms simply because she is a female author. Although it may be
true that women's writing tends to be read as offering a gender-specific
worldview more so than men's writing, I believe that this critical tendency
is not sufficient to explain the *contradictory* gendering of Sand's life and
fiction by the reading public as well as by literary critics.

We can understand the contradictory nature of Sandian criticism, I propose, only if we first understand the contradictions of gender encoded in
Sand's fiction itself. In order to do so, we must begin by rejecting the single

dialectical logic that has led readers and critics to position Sand's narratives on one side or the other of the sexual divide. Indeed, the sum of Sandian criticism indicates a sense of "androgynous" confusion, rather than clear feminine or masculine stereotyping. We would be in a better position to understand the complexity of Sand's fiction, I would argue, if we read her narratives as observing a double dialectical gendering process that also depends upon nineteenth-century understandings of class and race. As noted throughout this book, when read in terms of a double dialectics, each sex is defined negatively, as it externalizes characteristics associated with the other sex. At the same time, in a double dialectics, each sex is also defined positively, on the basis of the unique role it plays in the modern social order. Androgyny, as I have also shown earlier, constitutes the next step or negation of this double dialectical process of gendering. An androgynous subject or text (doubly) negates both feminine and masculine codes, thus producing an identity or aesthetics that is neither masculine nor feminine.

By analyzing Sand's idealism through the optic of androgyny, we can understand not only the formal organization of *Indiana,* but also Sand's ideological stance toward the nineteenth-century suffragette movement. As we remember, Sand refused to affiliate herself with the kind of feminist politics that sought to give women the same civic rights as men. Such an apparently antifeminist position, however, seems a lot more congruous with Sand's otherwise feminist criticisms of patriarchal institutions if we evaluate both stances through the lens of her idealist critique of existing gender norms. Rather than trying to transform women into the same kinds of citizen-subjects as men, Sand transforms both men and women into new and exemplary "androgynous" subjects. Let me pause to explain very briefly the way in which I believe Sand's critique of gender interacts with her idealist aesthetics.

First, it is important to note that what critics have called Sand's "idealist aesthetics" must be differentiated from "idealism" in the philosophical sense. Philosophically, idealism generally refers to a theory according to which objects have no existence apart from the mind or, otherwise phrased, objects of perception are only "ideas." Modern versions of idealist philosophy, originally attributable to the eighteenth-century philosopher George Berkeley, gained widespread cultural currency throughout Europe during the eighteenth and nineteenth centuries with the works of the German idealists, including Kant, Schiller, and Hegel. As Schor has argued, however, Sand's poetics bear a closer resemblance both to the idealist aesthetics of Hippolyte Taine[9] and, more generally, to the colloquial understanding of idealism as the elaboration of high moral aims.[10]

In her autobiographical and fictional works, Sand associates the idealization of characters with their transformative social power.[11] Only an ideal character type, Sand implies, may be able to set an example that would give life to utopian social visions that, quite literally, have "no place" in her society:[12]

> According to this [idealist] theory, the novel should be poetic, as well as an analytical work. It must have characters and situations that are true to life— even based on real life—that form a grouping around a type whose function is to embody the sentiment or main idea of the book. This character-type generally embodies in some way the passion of love . . . that passion, consequently that character-type, must be idealized . . . one must not be afraid to endow it with exceptional importance, powers beyond the ordinary, or subject it to delight or suffering that completely surpass the habitual, human ones, and that even surpass what most intelligent people think is believable.[13]

According to Sand's definition, idealism does not necessarily function as a contrast to the kinds of writing that claim verisimilitude. On the contrary, by maintaining that a novel "must have characters and situations that are true to life," Sand bases her idealism upon realist aesthetics. At the same time, contrary to what critics such as Proudhon assert about the digressive nature of Sand's writing, she proposes to extract the essential aspects of these characters by grouping them around "a type whose function is to embody the sentiment or main idea of the book." In Sand's idealist writing, then, one character represents an exemplary passion, assumes "an exceptional importance," and acquires powers "beyond the ordinary" in order to identify social visions that "surpass the habitual" range of identities, institutions, and mores. Only by moving beyond existing social codes, Sand implies, can her characters set an example that may influence readers to change their behavior.[14]

Indiana, in the novel by the same name, represents such an exemplary character. What makes Indiana a new model of human identity, as I have suggested, is the fact that she overcomes both the male and female roles of her (fictional) context by means of what is a double dialectical or androgynous process. In addition, my reading will emphasize more than Schor's and other influential studies of Sand's works the manner in which the social categories of class and race inflect the gendering process in *Indiana*. The male characters, and particularly Indiana's aristocratic lover Raymon de Ramière, assess Indiana's bourgeois femininity by constantly comparing her, at first favorably and then unfavorably, with the feminine characteristics of her Creole servant, Noun.

During the first part of the novel, he evaluates Noun's femininity—and finds it lacking in good taste—according to the model provided by Indiana's bourgeois standards. After Noun's suicide, however, Raymon sets up Noun's self-sacrificial femininity as the model that the proud Indiana must emulate. Evaluated by this standard, Indiana is found lacking. Class and race thus continually inflect and alter Raymon's understanding of gender. In the words of Anne McClintock, "Race and class difference cannot, I believe, be understood as sequentially derivative of sexual difference, or vice versa. Rather, the formative categories of imperial modernity are articulated categories in the sense that they come into being in historical relation to each other and emerge only in dynamic, shifting and intimate interdependence."[15] When judged by gender standards that apply to aristocratic women, however, both Indiana and Noun are found deficient in femininity. The novel does not treat this gender trouble as a failure, but rather as a success. Only her failure to perform gender—and hence her double difference from the men in the novel and the kinds of women they desire—renders Indiana an exemplary androgynous figure capable of transforming social convention. Let us now turn to the novel itself and examine how it develops the figure of Indiana by means of a double dialectical narrative process intended to subvert the social constructs of its times.

THE DIALECTICS OF GENDER: THE DIVISION OF SPHERES BETWEEN HUSBAND AND WIFE

The novel[16] begins by staging a gender-based contrast between two central characters. The male character, former lieutenant Delmare, appears as a man past his prime and forgotten by society: "But the glorious days had passed, when Lieutenant Delmare inhaled triumph with the air of the camps" (3–4). Being too old and out of touch with contemporary society to be defined in terms of his civic status in the masculine public sphere—the status relegated to the male subject—"the retired officer, forgotten now by an ungrateful country, was condemned to undergo all the consequences of marriage" (4). Like a woman, the retired lieutenant is "condemned" to a domestic civic identity and, more specifically, to his private role as husband.

The narrative, however, makes it clear that, as a man, M. Delmare has civic (property and marital) rights that Mme Delmare, as a woman, lacks under the existing Napoleonic Code. We find that "He was the husband of a young and pretty wife, the proprietor of a commodious manor with its appurtenances, and, furthermore, a manufacturer who had been fortunate in his undertakings" (4). Consequently, the fact that he has been deprived of his military and political functions does not necessarily strip M. Delmare of all of his privileges as a male citizen-subject. His rights over his wife confer upon him the civic power in the domestic sphere that he has lost in the public sphere. Early in the narrative, Sand's novel launches a critique of the institution of marriage as one that confirms the citizen status of men by denying it to women. The previous passage indicates that Mme Delmare counts as one of a series of objects, which include a manor and its dependents, owned by M. Delmare, the citizen–husband. Without property rights over such objects—and, furthermore, without placing woman among them—M. Delmare would have no civic status after his withdrawal from the masculine public sphere.

In addition, the wide, but not uncommon, discrepancy between the husband's and wife's ages helps maintain their asymmetrical relationship. This age difference relegates Mme Delmare to a filial legal status and M. Delmare to a paternal one. "For," the novel continues to explain, "his wife was nineteen years of age, and . . . if you had seen her, slender, pale, depressed, with her elbow resting on her knee, a mere child in that ancient household, beside that old husband, . . . you would have pitied Colonel Delmare's wife, and the colonel even more perhaps than his wife" (4). The relationship between husband and wife therefore entails a series of interdependent social contrasts: between citizen and dependent; between age and youth; between masculinity and femininity.

At the same time, however, these binary oppositions appear to be potentially unstable. Readers should pity the husband as much as the wife, the narrator urges, for there is a shared vulnerability between the wife's delicate youth and the husband's age; a common sadness that comes from the lack of marital rapport. Both members of the couple, defined by a dialectical process as cultural opposites, constitute a failure not only in terms of gender roles—since he is too old and infirm to count as a desirable bourgeois husband and she too young, nervous, and frail to count as a desirable bourgeois wife—but also in terms of the institution of marriage, which is supposed to unite such gender oppositions in a stable, whole, and androgynous union.[17]

To complicate matters further, the narrative attributes Mme Delmare's sadness, paleness, and almost *maladive* sensibility not only to the flawed and asymmetrical institution of marriage, but also to her cultural origins. Because she is a Creole from the Island of Bourbon, the narrator explains,

> Madame Delmare had all the superstitions of a nervous, sickly Creole; certain nocturnal sounds, certain phases of the moon were to her unfailing presages of specific events, of impending misfortunes, and the night spoke to that dreamy, melancholy creature a language full of mysteries and phantoms which she alone could understand and translate according to her fears and her sufferings. (14)

The marital hierarchy between M. and Mme Delmare interacts with and indeed shapes their "racial" difference. Just as the husband's civic identity was produced by elaborating the wife's lack of civic identity, so, too, the social attributes associated with his European heritage acquire meaning only in relation to her Creole heritage. A Creole identity, the novel assumes, entails a cultural heritage governed by mysticism and superstition. In contrast with such practices, European culture takes on a rationality that helps justify the imperialist ventures of Western nations.[18] As it reproduces such cultural stereotypes, however, *Indiana* does not endorse them. Not only does the novel criticize the practice of slavery, but also the idealism of the heroine itself depends upon her identification with those who are subject to European imperialism. What is wrong with such a sentimental identification?

MISTRESS AND SERVANT: THE DIALECTICS OF CLASS AND RACE

While Indiana may identify with the racially subordinated, she does not count fully as one of them. As we will observe, in her relations with her servant Noun, Indiana's class and even her racial status—as a white Creole—give her power and privilege over other colonized subjects. As the narrative unfolds we see that Indiana gains civic status only when, like her husband, she is defined in contrast to other kinds of subjects who have even less power than she does. The ambiguity that characterizes Indiana's Creole identity is not unique to Sand's novel. During the eighteenth and nineteenth centuries, the concept of "Creoleness" both distinguished and obfuscated the cultural boundaries between European and non-European, between colonizer and colonized.

According to the *Oxford Encyclopedic Dictionary,* "Creole" refers to a descendant of European, and particularly Spanish or French, settlers in the West Indies and North, Central, or South America. The term also refers to a person of mixed European and black descent.[19] On the one hand, "Creole" seems to refer only to national citizenship, distinguishing between Europeans born in Europe and those born in the colonies. As Benedict Anderson explains, "Even if he [a Creole] was born within one week of his father's migration, the accident of birth in the Americas consigned him to subordination—even though in terms of language, religion, ancestry or manners he was largely indistinguishable from the Spain-born Spaniard."[20] On the other hand, the term also serves to differentiate European from non-European ethnic backgrounds. Christopher L. Miller aptly characterizes the confusing polysemousness of "Creoleness": "The word thus speaks of a double differentiation or exile and opens the question of race while directly providing no answer to it."[21] It remains unclear, in other words, whether or not the term *Creole* functions to produce racial, national, or both kinds of distinctions. Similarly, the term may indicate not only the cultural domination of Creoles by European powers, but also the domination of some Creoles by others. Engaged in a subordinate relationship to citizens of the metropolis, the Creole of European heritage was also engaged in a dominant relationship to those who were defined as "Creole" according to both nationality and race.[22]

As a female Creole of Spanish and aristocratic lineage, then, Indiana's complex social status cannot be described in terms of simple oppositions between subordinate and dominant groups. The novel makes readers aware of Indiana's power by depicting her relationship to her fellow Creole servant, Noun. While Indiana may count as one of the Creole Europeans of ambiguous social status in the metropolis, Noun, "Madame Delmare's Creole maid" (15), has a much more clearly defined subordinate role. When introducing Noun, the novel describes the cultural and familial characteristics shared by Indiana and her double. We find out that "Noun was Madame Delmare's foster-sister; the two young women had been brought up together and loved each other dearly" (15). From the beginning, however, the differences in racial and class background between Noun and Indiana undermine their common emotive and familial ground. Their similarities, henceforth, will serve to further accentuate their social differences. We are told,

> Noun was tall and strong, glowing with health, active, alert, overflowing with ardent, passionate creole blood; and she far outshone with her resplendent beauty the frail and pallid charms of Madame Delmare; but the tenderness of their hearts and the strength of their attachment killed every feeling of feminine rivalry. (15)

This passage contrasts two types of femininity. Mme Delmare's social distinction, minimally described in terms of her "frail and pallid charms," emerges as a sign of bourgeois femininity only by virtue of its difference from the robustness of her servant, who, we are told, is "overflowing with ardent, passionate creole blood." A reading of gender codes thus elaborated indicates that, despite the significant conceptual and historical differences that separate race from class and gender, such cultural attributes cannot be understood apart from one another. It is precisely the difference between Noun's and Indiana's class and racial background that brands these women as representatives of different types of femininity.

The passage we have just examined ends proleptically on an ironic note. We are told that in spite of the differences in social status that distinguish these two women and subordinate one to the other, there was no rivalry between them. As we find out from reading the rest of the novel, however, it is precisely their rivalry—or love for the same man—that will separate Indiana and Noun. Such rivalry transforms this relationship into something at once much more and much less than a love triangle. On a semiotic level, the manner in which their lover, Raymon de Ramière, evaluates and chooses one woman over the other at different points in the narrative serves to distinguish which gender characteristics, inflected as they are by cultural assumptions about class and race, will become a sign of true, desirable femininity. By the end of the novel, Raymon rejects both women.

This action also has a larger narrative and cultural significance than the apparent fact that it constitutes a sad love story. I propose two lines of interpretation for this ending. First, I plan to show that the manner in which Noun and Indiana cope with Raymon's rejection distinguishes the prosaic from the idealized character. Noun's despair, culminating in her suicide, indicates, despite Raymon's self-serving interpretation, not self-sacrifice but rather weakness of resolve. By contrast, Indiana's decision to survive personal trauma and devote her life to freeing invalid slaves consolidates her status as an exemplary figure.[23] The novel thus idealizes Indiana by de-idealizing the figure of Noun. It is because Indiana did not react like Noun to Raymon's rejection, we are led to believe, that she gains credibility as an idealist heroine.[24]

Second, I interpret the fact that Raymon, the male protagonist, rejects both the bourgeois wife (albeit of aristocratic lineage) and the servant as a sign that, in the end, the novel endorses neither woman as a model of femininity. Being neither masculine nor feminine, neither European nor non-European, Indiana and Noun seem liminal and thus potentially disruptive figures in a European context. Sand's narrative obviously endorses such figures as having the potential to change undesirable social norms. The very fact that these women do not reproduce the existing social categories, that their cultural heritage and, in Noun's case, class background place them outside of and in opposition to those categories, lends the two heroines an elevated status.

Noun's suicide, however, eventually deprives her of the transcendent identity required by Sand's idealist poetics and politics. This contrast is in many ways predetermined by class and racial hierarchies well before the conclusion of the novel. Earlier I suggested that the novel establishes Indiana's ambiguous position as both colonizer and colonized, privileged and restricted by means of a double dialectical logic. This process contrasts her first with the male citizen-subjects of the novel and marks her as a noncitizen only to distinguish her from her servant and thus reestablish the very civic authority it took away.[25] The love triangle consisting of Raymon, Noun, and Indiana represents this double logic of gender as part and parcel of nineteenth-century theories of class and race.

In the eyes of the men in the novel, Indiana and Noun are differentiated, paradoxically, on the basis of how well they function as doubles who
can be mistaken for one another. When M. Delmare catches Raymon scal-
ing the walls of his property in an attempt to flee, he shoots him and
wounds him on the assumption that Raymon has been visiting Mme
Delmare. When the jealous M. Delmare discovers that it was Noun and
not Indiana who was seeing Raymon, he feels greatly relieved:

> Colonel Delmare was by no means desirous of following the development
> of their liaison; so he retired as soon as he had made sure that his wife had
> not for an instant occupied the thoughts of the Almaviva of this adventure.
> He heard enough of it, however, to realize the difference between the love
> of poor Noun, who threw herself into the affair with all the vehemence of
> her passionate nature, and that of the well-born youth, who yielded to the
> impulse of a day without abjuring the right to resume his reason on the
> morrow.

Once he finds out that Mme Delmare has remained faithful to him, M.
Delmare feels reassured in his possession of his wife and, more specifically, of his wife's virtue. He does not, however, measure Noun's worth
by the same bourgeois standards of femininity that he applies to his wife.
Semiotically, Noun's behavior establishes, by way of contrast, his wife's
virtue. Unlike Noun, Mme Delmare "n'avait pas occupé un instant
l'Almaviva de cette aventure."

While setting Noun apart from the mistress for whom she was initially
mistaken, the novel similarly positions her in a dialectical relationship to
the man she loves. Having discovered the affair between his servant and
his aristocratic neighbor, M. Delmare immediately ascertains that Noun
loves Raymon sincerely, while Raymon is only exercising his class and
gender privileges over her body. The narrator confirms this asymmetrical, and semiotically contradictory, nature of their relationship when she
adds, as if by way of justification, "You will find it difficult to believe
perhaps that Monsieur de Ramière, a young man of brilliant intellect, con-
siderable talents and many estimable qualities, accustomed to salon tri-
umphs and to adventures in perfumed boudoirs, had conceived a very
durable passion for the housekeeper in the household of a small manufacturer in Brie" (27). Voicing common class prejudices, the narrator cen-
sures not so much Raymon's sexual liaison with Noun as the fact that it
could have emotional implications and familial consequences. As the narrator continues to explain, "We have said that he was intelligent—that is
to say, he appreciated the advantages of birth at their real value" (28).

Translating this cultural commonplace into the complex dialectical play
of the novel, we could say that just as Indiana's bourgeois status depended

upon distinguishing itself as virtue in relation to Noun's lack thereof, so Raymon's aristocratic status distinguishes itself as power in relation to Noun's powerlessness (expressed in terms of her genuine vulnerability and love). Both forms of difference, we are led to conclude, must create asymmetries if the social fabric is to remain intact. Noun's dangerous sensual hold over Raymon poses a threat to the class system. Certainly, the narrator claims, rationally speaking, Raymon values the qualities of aristocratic culture. When overwhelmed by Noun's sensual Creole nature, however, he momentarily lapses into a passion that threatens to collapse class distinctions:

> He was a man of high principle when he argued with himself; but vehement passions often carried him beyond the bounds of his theories. At such times he was incapable of reflection, or he avoided appearing before the tribunal of conscience: he went astray, as if without his own knowledge, and the man of yesterday strove to deceive him of tomorrow. (28)

Although subordinated by and in some ways external to European society, the Creole servant represents a liminal figure who can transgress the social boundaries maintaining her inferiority. For this reason, as McClintock explains, female servants were placed in a paradoxical social position: "[W]omen who were ambiguously placed on the imperial divide (nurses, nannies, governesses, prostitutes and servants) served as boundary markers and mediators. Tasked with the purification and maintenance of boundaries, they were especially fetishized as dangerously ambiguous and contaminating" (*Imperial Leather*, 48). How does Raymon—and perhaps the novel itself—resist such contamination? I propose that by employing the figure of Noun as a negative foil that accentuates Indiana's legitimacy as a feminine citizen-subject, the narrative wards off some of the cultural dangers posed by female servants.

Raymon himself relies upon the figure of Indiana, and more generally upon aristocratic conventions, to defeminize the servant with whom he risks falling in love. First and foremost, his mother embodies a femininity against which he will (unfavorably) measure not only Noun, but also Indiana. Raymon owes his sense of social discernment, the narrator explains, "to his mother . . . , whose superior intelligence, sparkling conversation and private virtues made her an exceptional woman. It was from her that he inherited those excellent principles which always led him back to the right path and prevented him, despite the impetuosity of his twenty-five years, from ever forfeiting his claim to public esteem" (34). Sobered by the thoughts of the social conventions he respects, Raymon speculates,

> The wife of a peer of France who should sacrifice herself so recklessly would be a priceless conquest; but a lady's maid! That which is heroism in the one

becomes brazen-faced effrontery in the other. With the one a world of jealous rivals envies you; with the other a rabble of scandalized flunkeys con-
demns you. The lady of quality sacrifices twenty previous lovers to you; the
lady's maid sacrifices only a husband that she might have had. (30–31)

Raymon obviously abides by the logic of an older and increasingly dated
model of courtship. According to this aristocratic model, a woman's worth
is measured not so much by her virtue—the bourgeoise's cultural capital—as by her refusal of the customary lovers. Pursuing this line of
thought, Raymon concludes that Noun has nothing to offer him in exchange for his love. She has indeed offered him her body, but according
to cultural practice, that was something Raymon was already entitled to
obtain at no cost. Raymon interprets Noun's inability to reciprocate as a
reflection of her lack of femininity. By implication, only an aristocratic or
a bourgeois woman could be feminine. As the narrator declares quite
bluntly, if ironically, "What can you expect? Raymon was a man of fash-
ionable morals, of elegant manners, of poetic passion. In his eyes a grisette
was not a woman, and Noun, by virtue of a beauty of the first order, had
taken him by surprise on a day of popular merrymaking" (31). Seen in
contrast with her "un-feminine" servant and foil, Indiana initially appears
as the very embodiment of the femininity that Raymon desires. Let us now
follow the narrative process that first establishes, and then undermines,
Indiana's status as an exemplary feminine figure.

When an acquaintance draws his attention to Indiana and recounts her
genealogy at a ball, Raymon feels initially reassured by her class position:

"That young woman," said a woman who knew everybody and who played
the part of an almanac at social functions, "is the daughter of that old fool,
De Carvajal, who tried to play Joséphin, and who died ruined at Ile Bourbon. This lovely exotic flower has made a foolish marriage, I believe; but her
aunt stands well at court." (37)

Despite its positive tone, one can detect ambivalence in this description.
The account of Indiana's aristocratic and Spanish lineage cannot offset
either her bourgeois marriage or her Creole and (as we recall from
Anderson's description) somehow less than European colonial origins.
The moment when Raymon approaches Indiana, whose very name accentuates the non-Western element of her cultural heritage, calls to mind the
opening scene of the novel, which attributes Indiana's unsettling sadness
as much to her marriage as to her Creole background:

Raymon had drawn near the fair Indian. A peculiar emotion seized him
every time that he looked at her; he had seen that pale, sad face; perhaps in
some dream . . . Raymon's gaze disturbed her who was the object of it; she

was awkward and shy, like a person unaccustomed to society, and the sensation that she caused seemed to embarrass rather than to please her. (38)

This time, however, Indiana's "pale and sad face" evokes yet another scene in the novel, when she awakens her husband's suspicion by taking care of the wounded and unconscious Raymon after her husband shoots him. Immediately following this suggestive identification between Noun and Indiana, who are in fact the two "belles Indiennes" tending to Raymon's wounds, the novel proceeds to differentiate them according to Raymon's aristocratic standards. After having seen Indiana at the ball in all her modesty and splendor, "The next morning he had completely forgotten Noun. All that he knew about her was that she belonged to Madame Delmare" (41). As we recall from the earlier scene in which Mme Delmare was described as her husband's property, this means of describing a person as an object that belongs to another establishes the subjectivity of the "owner." Just as M. Delmare gained a civic identity in relation to Indiana's dependency, so Indiana gains subjective status as Noun descends to the status of nonsubject.

Having rejected Noun, however, Raymon feels unable to abandon his romantic or sexual relations with either the servant or her mistress. It is as if he needs the increasingly abject figure of Noun to heighten, by comparison, his appreciation for Indiana. Telling each woman in turn that he loves only her, Raymon rationalizes his duplicitous conduct by means of a binary hierarchy between body and soul. That is to say, he satisfies his carnal desire with Noun in order to maintain the purity of his spiritual love for Madame Delmare. By eliminating sensual contact from his relationship with Indiana, Raymon momentarily succeeds in elevating his feelings for her to a higher spiritual plane. "Although his conduct at this crisis seems two-faced and treacherous," the narrator claims, "his heart was sincere, and had always been. He had loved Noun with his senses; he loved Madame Delmare with all his heart" (57). In Raymon's eyes, and in the semiotics of the novel by and large, the figure of Noun is essential in constituting Indiana as a model of desirable femininity.

After seeing Indiana at the ball, Raymon not only classifies the two women, but also establishes a metonymical relation between their belongings and their class distinction. When Raymon enters Mme Delmare's bedroom to meet with Noun, he initially mistakes the servant for the mistress. To entice him and enhance her own beauty, Noun, in one of the many doubling scenes of the novel, had put on Indiana's clothes. It is not so much (what might be called) Noun's travesty of class, however, that initially confuses Raymon. He is deceived instead by the very surroundings that are imbued with the order, cleanliness, and simplicity of the bourgeoisie:

> The exquisite taste and simplicity which characterized the furniture; . . . and,
> above all, the little bed half-hidden behind its muslin curtains, as white and
> modest as a maiden's bed . . . all these revealed the presence of Madame
> Delmare, and Raymon was seized with a strange thrill as he thought that
> that cloak-enveloped woman who had led him thither might be Indiana
> herself. (59–60)

In initially mistaking Noun for Indiana, Raymon is not fooled by Noun's
ruse so much as led by his characteristically dialectical way of thinking
that produces distinctions between women on the basis of race and class.
Regarding a bourgeoise (Indiana) as the contrary of a servant (Noun),
Raymon assumes that anything associated with Indiana cannot belong to
Noun and vice versa. In other words, he cannot conceive of Noun as a
participant in the high bourgeois world he associates with Indiana. Nor
can he conceive of Noun as fitting, not only physically but also socially,
into Mme Delmare's elegant and simple clothes. For him, the clean room
and the modest attire metonymically represent the chaste Indiana, just as,
by contrast, the servant's quarters and the immodest clothes represent the
unchaste Noun.[26] Precisely because he draws such a sharp class distinction between the two women, where each one is defined as the negation
of the characteristics associated with the other, Raymon can be fooled by
Noun's impersonation of Indiana. Once again, however, the momentary
narrative fusion of the two women establishes the basis on which they will
become more sharply distinguished:

> But it was only a momentary error—Indiana would have concealed her
> charms more carefully; her modest bosom would have been visible only
> through the triple gauze veil of her corsage; she would perhaps have dressed
> her hair with natural camellias, but they would not have frisked about on
> her head in such seductive disorder; she might have encased her feet in satin
> shoes, but her chaste gown would not have betrayed thus shamelessly the
> mysteries of her shapely legs. (60)

In every respect, Noun serves as a measure of sexual excess—in dress,
ornaments, and sensuality—which Raymon interprets as a lack of proper
femininity. The two women cannot be mistaken for one another after all.
Even when wearing her mistress's clothes, Noun draws too much attention to her physical attributes. By contrast, Raymon speculates, Indiana
would have worn the same clothes with an opposite sense of fashion. She
would have understated her beauty rather than accentuating it; she would
have modestly hid her femininity, thus enhancing its cultural value all the
more. While reinforcing the role of clothes in drawing class boundaries,
however, Raymon's initial confusion of Noun for Indiana also underscores
the mutability of such codes. As McClintock explains, "[S]umptuary laws

contain an internal paradox, for the fact that class and rank are made legible by the wearing, or not wearing of 'cloth of gold, silk or purple' reveals the invented nature of social distinction, throwing into visibility the question of both the origins and the legitimacy of rank and power. The bits and pieces of colored cloth that are the legible insignia of degree are also permanently subject to disarrangement and symbolic theft" (*Imperial Leather*, 174). Rather than marking necessary class boundaries, sumptuary laws rely upon the successful performance of class roles.

INDIANA'S ANDROGYNY: THE CONSTRUCTION OF IDEALIST CHARACTERS AS NEITHER MASCULINE NOR FEMININE CITIZEN-SUBJECTS

Indiana's performance of sumptuary codes, however, is itself precarious because it is entirely dependent upon Noun's failure to perform them. Only by emphasizing Noun's failure can Indiana acquire a positive and valorized identity in Raymon's eyes. Such a dialectical understanding of the role played by class in constructing gender becomes even more obvious after Noun's suicide. Pregnant, abandoned by her lover, and chastised by her mistress—who, in yet another moment of narrative doubling, believes that Noun allowed Raymon in her room to dishonor her—Noun drowns herself in despair. Once Noun dies, Raymon will focus on the manner in which Mme Delmare, now lacking her dialectical foil, loses her ability to represent his feminine ideal. Consequently, in the second part of the novel, which makes a second move in a dialectical model of femininity, Mme Delmare becomes the negative standard of womanhood in contrast to (what Raymon belatedly regards as) Noun's properly self-sacrificial femininity.

Parenthetically, it is worth noting that the feminine identities of both Noun and Indiana are dialectically established not only in relation to one another along the axis of class, but also in relation to the men of the novel along that of gender. As mentioned earlier, the identity of the male citizen-subjects—M. Delmare, Raymon, and Ralph—emerges in relation to Indiana's exclusion from the public sphere. "Madame Delmare, ignorant as a genuine creole, had never dreamed hitherto of considering the momentous questions that were now discussed before her every day" (141). So far, the narrative seems to endorse a Hegelian vision of women as naturally intuitive and disinterested in civic affairs. In other words, the novel presents woman as the constitutive outside of the masculine citizen-subject. But the next line undermines the naturalization of such a vision.

It is not because women naturally lack civic virtue that they are disinterested in public affairs, the narrator argues, but because misogynist views and institutions educate them to be ignorant of political matters. As the narrator explains, "She had been brought up by Sir Ralph, who had a poor opinion of the intelligence and reasoning power of womankind, and who had confined himself to imparting some positive information likely to be of immediate use" (141). Such a description of woman's ethical vision as universal—guided by intuition rather than deliberation—once again appears to confirm the Hegelian dichotomy between women's universalist ethics and men's simultaneously particularist and universalist ethics. Rather than endorsing Hegel's dialectics of gender, however, Sand reproduces that logic in order to overturn its hierarchy and privilege the heroine's intuitive faculties:

> Indiana opposed to the interests of civilization, when raised to the dignity of principles of action, the straightforward ideas and simple laws of good sense and humanity; her arguments were characterized by an unpolished freedom which sometimes embarrassed Raymon and always charmed him by its childlike originality. (142)

In this passage, the transition in narrative voice—from the narrator's to Raymon's—marks a shift in the value attributed to Indiana's intuitive ethics. While the narrator appears to valorize feminine ethics, Raymon dismisses it as charming and infantile in order to validate his own political views. Following this logic, it is not surprising that even after Noun's death, Indiana's qualities provide a contrast that rejuvenates Raymon's masculine role as an active citizen in the public sphere. After interacting with her, Raymon launches himself into a promising career as a journalist specializing in political analysis:

> Thus Raymon had no sooner returned to that society, which was his element and his home, than he felt its vital and exciting influences. The petty love affairs that had engrossed him vanished for a moment in the face of broader and more brilliant interests. (95)

Employing Hegel's scheme, we might say that once Raymon has fulfilled his particular love for Indiana, he moves back to the "broader and more brilliant" masculine public sphere.

So far I have argued that precisely because Indiana's contributions to the political discussions among men appear to them as ignorant, their identities as masculine citizen-subjects become more firmly consolidated in opposition to hers. I have also suggested that the narrator seems to undermine such a Hegelian description of citizenship and gender, or at least overturn its hierarchies and valorize the feminine subject and its supposedly universalist ethics. It would appear that such an inversion of the values does not change the underlying binary structure between masculine and feminine ethics, or between private and public spheres. I maintain, however, that the novel critiques such gender distinctions. In fact, the male characters appear less than ideal—or as improper citizen-subjects—precisely because of their formulaic conformity to the division of spheres. Alluding to M. Delmare's brutality toward his wife, the narrator asks:

> Do you know what they call an *honnête homme* in the provinces? . . . He is a man who does not encroach on his neighbor's field . . . Provided that he religiously respects the lives and purses of his fellow-citizens, nothing more is demanded of him. He may beat his wife, maltreat his servants, ruin his children, and it is nobody's business. Society punishes only those acts which are injurious to it; private life is beyond its jurisdiction. (96)

According to the narrator, the distinction between domestic and public spheres only serves to protect men's domination of all those whom they "possess" in the private sphere, including their wives, children, and servants. While in the masculine public sphere laws render individuals accountable for their misconduct, by defining the private sphere in a dialectical fashion as external to civil society, men are not held accountable for unethical behavior toward women and other dependents. As we return to the analysis of the manner in which Raymon's assumptions about class serve to de-idealize Mme Delmare's femininity following Noun's death, it helps to keep in mind that, given the novel's critique of gender roles, the process of defeminization transforms Indiana from an ordinary bourgeoise into an exemplary androgynous heroine. In other words, the further Indiana deviates from Raymon's vision of her as a desirable woman, the closer she comes to this new ideal of the androgynous woman who can play the kind of transformative civic role endorsed by the novel.

Following Noun's death, Raymon's relationship with Indiana becomes more intimate. At this point he discovers that his image of her was mostly a projection of his own desires. For instance, when he goes hunting with Indiana and her cousin Ralph, Raymon is taken aback by her incredible force and fearlessness:

> Nor did he suspect that in that frail and apparently timid woman there abode a more than masculine courage. . . . So much determination alarmed him and nearly disgusted him with Madame Delmare. Men, especially lovers, are addicted to the innocent fatuity of preferring to protect weakness rather than to admire courage in womankind. Shall I confess it? Raymon was terrified at the promise of high spirit and tenacity in love which such intrepidity seemed to afford. It was not like the resignation of poor Noun, who

preferred to drown herself rather than to contend against her misfortunes. (128–129)

Once he begins to interact with Indiana—rather than simply contrast her with Noun from a distance—Raymon observes that she does not conform to any of the stereotypes he had attributed to her. While seeming frail and feminine, Indiana has a moral and physical force that is both unfeminine (according to his conceptions of femininity) and unmasculine (since he regards her courage as "more than masculine"). Furthermore, because Raymon understands gender as a single dialectical relation, the fact that Indiana fails to confirm gender differences destabilizes his own sense of masculinity, which depended upon a contrast between her frailty and his strength. Such a contrast, the narrator implies, is a cultural myth that consolidates a historically specific division of spheres. Assuming this myth to be based on nature, Raymon—rather than appreciating Indiana's courage—begins to situate Indiana in opposition to what he now regards as Noun's properly feminine resignation. While Indiana might have been the better woman in terms of class, Noun is the better woman in terms of gender.

Once she notices that Raymon wants to treat her as he did Noun and consummate their love, Indiana resists his advances. In order to forewarn Raymon of the potential consequences of a sexual—as opposed to purely romantic—relationship between them, she dresses in Noun's clothes. This doubling, like the figure of the chiasmus itself, is inversely symmetrical to an earlier scene of cross-dressing in the novel. While Noun had donned Indiana's dress to excite Raymon's passion, Indiana dresses in Noun's clothes to cool his desire. As in the earlier scene, Raymon enters Indiana's bedroom in semidarkness, where he finds a barely visible female figure dressed in a servant's clothes, her head covered by the scarf Noun had worn on the night of her suicide. The effect of his misrecognition is the anticipated one: "Raymon, fairly overcome by terror, nearly fell backward, thinking that his superstitious fancies were realized" (162).

Mme Delmare does not stop, however, at delivering this minor shock. She carries the power of metonymic logic even further as she gives Raymon Noun's locks of hair and tells him that they represent her own sacrifice to him. When he passes the hair through his fingers, Raymon recognizes Noun's chevelure, "of an Ethiopian black, of an Indian texture, of a lifeless heaviness" (163). Conceptualizing the difference between the two women as a dialectical relationship between dead and alive, victim and tormentor, weakness and strength, Raymon decides once and for all that Noun's lack of power, which was always for him a sign of femininity, is preferable to Indiana's excessive strength. "Poor Noun!" he exclaims,

It was she whom I treated badly, not you . . . She took her own life in order
to leave me a future. She sacrificed herself to my repose. You are not the
woman to have done as much, madame! . . . Ah! when I spurned so devoted
a love to take up with so savage a passion as yours, I was no less mad than
guilty. (164–165)

From this point on, Raymon wishes to conquer Indiana's virtue not "from
a feeling of pride but in a revengeful spirit" (172). Only by means of such
masculine conquest can he hope to render Indiana properly submissive
and then abandon her much as he had Noun.

   During the rest of the novel Indiana spends part of her youth trying to
conform to the figure of the self-sacrificing woman that Raymon desires.
Yet her actions remain unconvincing. Raymon eventually marries the
woman who seemed destined for him from the very beginning. His young
wife combines a taste for aristocratic culture (that neither Noun nor Indiana could satisfy) with a resignation to existing social codes. In an ironic
twist, however, the novel illustrates that the ideal of submissive femininity that Raymon had searched for is nowhere to be found. Mlle de Nangy
may have been both aristocratic and a believer in social hierarchy, but
these attributes did not make her into a submissive wife. On the contrary,

Mademoiselle de Nangy was fully resolved, therefore, to submit to marriage
as a social necessity; but she took a malicious pleasure in making use of the
liberty which still belonged to her, and in imposing her authority for some
time on the man who aspired to deprive her of it . . . For her, life was a matter
of stoical calculation, happiness a childish delusion against which she must
defend herself as a weakness and an absurdity. (271–272)

Raymon's class ideal of gender, when juxtaposed with Noun's and
Indiana's idealized passions, ironically appears as just one more example
of the prosaic emotional bonds that characterize socially acceptable relations between men and women. As we have seen, Sand's novel subjects
such relations to relentless critique.

   The only way for a woman such as Indiana to fulfill her idealist civic
visions, the conclusion of the story suggests, is to return to a cultural space
beyond the reach of the codes governing her society. As mentioned, in the
second version of the novel, Indiana and Ralph devote their lives not so
much to fulfilling a role in French culture, but to altering it by freeing the
slaves of their native island, thus challenging the nationalist and imperialist versions of citizenship that were gaining currency in European societies. This action, which negotiates the borders between European citizens
and Creole (non)citizens, enables Indiana once again to cross racial, class,
and sexual boundaries. As we have seen, the male characters in the novel,

with the sole exception of Ralph, are ultimately disappointed with what they consider Indiana's lack of proper femininity. The logic of *Indiana*, however, indicates that it is precisely Indiana's failure to conform to the dominant social institutions of her context that makes her an exemplary heroine prepared to carry through utopian projects of social reform. Sand's idealist experimentation with exemplary character types who move beyond nineteenth-century cultural norms manifests, in the words of Schor,

> her refusal to reproduce mimetically and hence to legitimize a social order inimical to the disenfranchised, and among them women. . . . To recanonize Sand thus requires nothing less than a reconsideration of realism as it constructs and supports the phallo- and ethnocentric social order we so often confuse with reality. Finally, to recanonize Sand will call for an elaboration of a poetics of the ethical.[27]

A poetics of the ethical, for Sand, is inseparable from the politics of gender, class, and race. Such a politics, I have tried to suggest, begins and ends with the representation of androgynous character types who are simultaneously internal and external to the binary codes of sexual, class, and racial differences. As we have seen, the double dialectical logic of *Indiana* indicates that there is no ready-made utopian space that is completely external to gender or other kinds of social constructs. To create a more modest, liminal space that both relies upon and violates social convention, Sand's novel develops an androgynous heroine: a heroine who is neither masculine nor feminine, but whose (negative) sexual identity is shaped by the civic codes that form both masculine and feminine citizen-subjects. Only once Indiana is assessed by and found lacking according to binary representations of gender—which invariably intersect with class and racial codes—does she become a figure capable of elaborating both a poetics and a politics of the ethical.

Sand's fiction offers a logical point of departure for twentieth-century "second-wave" feminism: a feminism, in other words, that positions itself in an ambivalent relation to sexual difference. On the one hand, like Sand, contemporary feminist scholars acknowledge that there are no simple ways to negate discourses of sexual difference without at the same time failing to address the social asymmetries between men and women. On the other hand, they also attempt to find a partially external, or what I have called "androgynous" space, from which to transform gender codes. My next and final chapter, which focuses upon Foucault's reading of Herculine Barbin's journal and several contemporary feminist critiques of this reading, brings nineteenth-century debates about gender and citizenship into the twentieth century.

NOTES

1. Pierre Salomon's *George Sand* and Edith Thomas's *George Sand* provide excellent introductions to the critical responses generated by Sand's persona and fiction.

2. Sandy Petrey analyzes the gender ambiguity of George Sand's persona and fiction in "George and Georgina Sand: Realist Gender in *Indiana*," in *Sexuality and Textuality*.

3. Leslie Rabine offers a nuanced discussion of Sand's representations of femininity in "George Sand and the Myth of Femininity," in *Women and Literature*. For a discussion of Sand's ambiguous relation to the feminist movement, see Claudine Chonez's "George Sand et le féminisme," in *Europe*.

4. Naomi Schor discusses and critiques the contradictory readings of Sand's feminism or antifeminism (especially those performed by contemporary feminist critics) in her chapter "Idealism and Its Discontents" in *George Sand and Idealism*. As she recounts, "The episode is well known. In 1848, at the height of preelection fever, a group of feminists gathered at the Club de la Rue Taranne proposed the candidacy of Georges Sand to the National Assembly. Two days after the publication of that motion in La Voix des Femmes (April 6, 1848), George Sand sent a letter to the editors of *La Réforme* and *La Vraie République*, in which she curtly shoots down this ill-timed nomination. . . . Neither the tone nor the tenor of this text is designed to make Sand a heroine in the eyes of historians of French feminism, and it singularly complicates the task of those—both men and women— who insist on enlisting Sand as a feminist and making of her an ancestress of the contemporary women's movement. In fact, opposite this disturbing, not to say frankly antifeminist text, we could place other texts that are equally well known and clearly feminist, where Sand defends the equality of women before the law, clamors for the rights of women to divorce and to be educated, and castigates the patriarchal order and the unjust condition of women" (68–69).

5. In *George Sand and Idealism,* Schor not only illustrates that idealism and realism must be viewed in relation to one another, but also that idealism preceded and was considered more important than realism during the first part of the nineteenth century. As she explains, "Realism, cut off from idealism, is a radically decontextualized representational mode, a perennial trend rather than a historically specific literary, aesthetic, and political movement. Uncoupled from its binary other, realism is caught up in an endless semantic drift" (29).

6. For an analysis of the feminization and devalorization of the detail and the ornamental in aesthetic philosophy (beginning with neoclassical and ending with modernist aesthetics), see Naomi Schor's *Reading in Detail: Aesthetics and the Feminine*.

7. Proudhon's aesthetic and social theories are also presented in *Du principe de l'art et de sa destination sociale*.

8. I will be citing from George Sand's *Indiana*, George Burnham Ives, tr. (New York: Howard Fertig, 1975).

9. See Hippolyte Taine's *Derniers essais de critique et d'histoire* and *Philosophie de l'art*.

10. In *George Sand and Idealism,* Schor persuasively argues not only that Sand's idealism differs from the tradition of speculative philosophy, but also why, despite and even because of its difference from masculine idealist theories, it must be considered an equally worthy object of study for literary and cultural analysis.

11. For a general discussion of idealism, see Nicolas Rescher's *Ethical Idealism: An Inquiry into the Nature and the Function of Ideals.*

12. Sand's conception of idealist utopia corresponds closely to the excellent definition offered by Darko Suvin in *Metamorphoses of Science Fiction: On the Poetics and History of a Literary Genre.* Suvin states, "Utopia is the verbal construction of a particular quasi-human community where sociopolitical institutions, norms, and individual relationships are organized according to a more perfect principle than in the author's community, this construction being based on estrangement arising out of an alternative historical hypothesis" (49).

13. Citation from *Histoire de ma vie* (922/2:161), found in *George Sand and Idealism,* 41.

14. Ernst Bloch analyzes the manner in which literature functions to critique and improve society in *The Utopian Function of Art and Literature: Selected Essays.*

15. McClintock, *Imperial Leather: Race, Gender and Sexuality in the Colonial Context,* 6.

16. I will be citing from George Sand's *Indiana,* George Burnham Ives, tr. (New York: Howard Fertig, 1975).

17. In *Androgyny and the Denial of Difference,* Kari Weil demonstrates that the concept of androgyny (in contrast to the more unstable concept of hermaphrodism) generally signified a stable union of gender opposites in Romantic literature.

18. Anderson, *Imagined Communities: Reflections on the Origin and Spread of Nationalism.*

19. *Oxford Encyclopedic English Dictionary,* 341.

20. Anderson, *Imagined Communities,* 57.

21. Miller, *Blank Darkness: Africanist Discourse in French,* 94.

22. According to Anderson, "For the first time the metropoles had to deal with—for that era—vast numbers of 'fellow-Europeans' (over three million in the Spanish Americas by 1800) far outside Europe. If the indigenes were conquerable by arms and disease, and controllable by the mysteries of Christianity and a completely alien culture (as well as, for those days, an advanced political organization), the same was not true of the creoles, who had virtually the same relationship to arms, disease, Christianity and European culture as the metropolitans. In other words, in principle, they had readily at hand the political, cultural and military means for successfully asserting themselves. They constituted simultaneously a colonial community and an upper class" (*Imagined Communities,* 57).

23. Sand wrote two endings to *Indiana.* In the first one, Indiana and her cousin Ralph commit suicide by throwing themselves into a cascade on their native island of Bourbon. In the second and more definitive conclusion, however, Indiana and Ralph devote themselves to freeing invalid Creole slaves. This second version establishes a much stronger contrast between Indiana's and Noun's reaction to hardship and heightens the sense of Indiana's "idealist," or better than real, persona.

24. Arlette Béteille offers an excellent analysis of Sand's multiple endings to *Indiana* in "Où finit Indiana? Problématique d'un dénouement," in *Recherches nouvelles: Groupe de recherches sur George Sand*.

25. As McClintock explains in *Imperial Leather*, "Colonized women, before the intrusions of imperial rule, were invariably disadvantaged within their societies, in ways that gave the colonial reordering of their sexual and economic labor different outcomes from those of colonized men. . . . Colonial women were also ambiguously placed within this process. Barred from the corridors of formal power, they experienced the privileges and social contradictions of imperialism very differently from colonial men. . . . As such, white women were not the hapless onlookers of empire but were ambiguously complicit both as colonizers and colonized, privileged and restricted, acted upon and acting" (6).

26. As McClintock illustrates in *Imperial Leather*, during the nineteenth century in England and also in France and other European nations, "Working-class women were figured as biologically driven to lechery and excess; upper-class women were naturally indifferent to the deliriums of the flesh. . . . The Victorian splitting of women into whores and Madonnas, nuns and prostitutes has its origins, then, not in universal archetype, but in the class structure of the household" (86–87).

27. Schor, *George Sand and Idealism*, 54.

5

Gender Trouble in the Diary of Herculine Barbin: Unreading Foucault

In 1980, Michel Foucault published an introduction to the journal of a nineteenth-century hermaphrodite named Herculine Barbin. This journal traces the experience of an individual, born in 1838 and deceased in 1868, whose life was eventually destroyed by sexual ambiguity. In an effort to impose what Foucault calls a "true sex" upon the hermaphrodite, doctors, lawyers, and priests compelled Herculine to undergo a sex-change operation that would transform her into a "man." No more comfortable with a male identity than she had been with her female one, Herculine/Abel eventually committed suicide.

Obviously, it is difficult to situate this journal within any disciplinary or generic categories. On a thematic level, Herculine's diary epitomizes the fascination with the hermaphrodite that we encounter in novels such as Théophile Gautier's *Mademoiselle de Maupin* and Honoré de Balzac's *Sarrasine, Béatrix,* and *La Cousine Bette.* As an autobiography, however, Herculine's diary must be granted a curious kind of literary status. During the eighteenth century, the memoir and the novel combined to produce one of the most popular genres, known as the memoir-novel, or in some cases, the epistolary-memoir-novel. The popularity of fictional works such as Richardson's *Pamela* or Françoise de Graffigny's *Lettres d'une Péruvienne* and of autobiographical narratives such as Rousseau's *Confessions* and Mme Roland's *Mémoires* obviously contributed to the modern autobiographical form, which often turns on sexual relationships.

By the nineteenth century, autobiography had come to offer, along with the bildungsroman, the model of subject formation. Precisely because of its questionable literary status, autobiography has become central to cultural critics who work in the tradition established by Foucault. Foucault, however, deliberately breaks with the kind of historiography that focuses on the memoirs of military and political figures to the neglect of auto-biographies. He privileges instead journals authored by individuals with no conventional claim to importance. According to Foucault, for the pur-pose of writing a history of sexuality, there can be no more important text than one documenting the formation of an individual of questionable sexuality. What better way to capture the moment when identity came to be grounded in the male body than by means of the diary of a hermaphro-dite who was medically ordained to become a man? Like Foucault, I, too, believe that such curious examples from what was a marginal genre are precisely where one must go to understand forms of thinking about sexu-ality and civic identity that are more naturalized in sophisticated literary works. Thus, I approach the diary of Herculine Barbin with the assump-tion that it is not an anomalous text but, on the contrary, symptomatic of the culture that produced Balzac and Flaubert.

In analyzing Herculine's diary, Foucault raises the following question: "Do we *truly* need a *true* sex?" To this question, he replies: "With a per-sistence that borders on stubbornness, modern Western societies have answered in the affirmative." He reads Herculine's diary to understand how and why indeed "Western societies have answered in the affirma-tive." By introducing us to this autobiographical account of no established literary value that describes the unhappy life of an otherwise insignificant person, Foucault provides cultural critics with privileged insight into a turning point of the history of sexuality:

> Here is a document drawn from that strange history of our "true sex." It is not unique, but it is rare enough. . . . The date, first of all. The years from around 1860–1870 were precisely one of those periods when investigations of sexual identity were carried out with the most intensity, in an attempt not only to establish the true sex of hermaphrodites but also to identify, clas-sify and characterize the different types of perversion.[1]

As does the *History of Sexuality*, Foucault's introduction to Herculine's journal critically examines the understanding of sexuality that we have inherited from our nineteenth-century predecessors. Such an understand-ing includes belief that "true sex" is a biological identity, that it takes only two mutually exclusive forms (male or female), and that this identity pro-vides a natural basis for social conventions or gender. Regarding sex as a prediscursive domain, Foucault insists, does not enable us to understand the history of sexuality. Such a history, in his estimation, investigates not only the codes of sexual conduct, but also the discourses that shape the material body.

Furthermore, according to Foucault, what is particularly interesting and unique about Herculine's diary—what enables it to expose the discourses that produce the notion of "a true sex"—is its peculiar self-contradictory representation of sexuality. At the same time that the text reproduces the premise of a natural or true unisexual identity, it also fundamentally questions the very foundations it presupposes. Both Herculine's journal and the experts' articles Foucault appends to the diary stage the cultural efforts to represent unisexual identity as natural even in a hermaphrodite, where such a representation would seem most implausible according to its own logic. Herculine's journal therefore catches modern society in the constitutive contradiction that it must hide in order for its representation of sexuality to remain compelling. That is, it captures the social effort to depict a hermaphrodite's identity as naturally either male or female even while engaged in the process of transforming Herculine's ambisexual identity into the male identity it should already have been. In so doing, it gives more credence to the notion that culture mediates what it takes to be purely natural rather than to its premise that culture is based upon nature.

Because of its ability to interrogate so effectively the very categories it proposes, we may assume, Foucault chooses Herculine's narrative as an object of historical analysis. By challenging the notion that having one true sex is a natural fact that determines social codes rather than the other way around, Foucault's reading also revolutionizes our own understanding of the distinction between sex and gender. Indeed, even though we think ourselves more tolerant than our Victorian forebears,

> Nevertheless, the idea that one must indeed finally have a true sex is far from being completely dispelled. . . . [W]e continue to think that some of these [deviant sexual identities and practices] are insulting to "the truth": we may be prepared to admit that a "passive" man, a "virile" woman, people of the same sex who love one another, do not seriously impair the established order; but are ready enough to believe that there is something like an "error" involved in what they do. An "error" as understood in the most traditionally philosophical sense: a manner of acting that is not adequate to reality. Sexual irregularity is seen as belonging more or less to the realm of chimeras. (x)

Foucault argues that today as much as during the nineteenth century, what establishes the truth of sexual identity is the process that declares everything that does not correspond to binary categories as less real and unnatural: in his words, as an error in reading the body.

The truth of biological sex, in turn, is used to legitimate gender-based norms, including those that establish codes of masculinity, femininity, and what has come to be called sexual orientation. Such codes, Foucault further demonstrates, are intimately tied to the practices of citizenship. They draw distinctions between legitimate citizen-subjects (those who conform to moral and sexual codes) and those who, like Herculine, belong to the many classes of "deviant" subjects that undermine the civic order. In his critique of the truth of sex, Foucault asks us to consider the following questions: What if both biological and social discourses contribute to the formation of what we take to be our natural sexual identities? What if, in addition, so-called deviant sexual identities and practices are no more and no less truthful than sexual norms?

According to Foucault's reading of Herculine's diary, the hermaphrodite's sexual confusion—as a person who combines the physical and behavioral characteristics of both sexes—offers the clearest proof, even in the face of empiricist readings of the body, that even when sex is not clear, it will be forced to conform with what is taken to be the nature of one sex or the other. The material and discursive processes that transform a hermaphrodite first into a woman and then into a man chart the discursive processes that make all of us fit sexual categories. Thus, Foucault uses the androgyne, or the supposed sexual exception, to explain how the rules of sexual difference are culturally produced and the role they play in the creation of modern citizenship.

FEMINIST REVISIONS OF FOUCAULT'S HISTORY OF SEXUALITY

Given that Foucault challenges the conceptions of sexuality that justify sexual differences and hierarchies, it is not surprising that numerous feminist critics employ Foucauldian theories as a means of understanding gender. Feminist critics such as Nancy Armstrong,[2] Sandra Bartky,[3] Judith Butler, Jana Sawicki,[4] Nancy Fraser,[5] Lois McNay,[6] and many others have used Foucault's insights into the history of sexuality to undermine the argument that gender roles are natural. McNay, for example, finds helpful Foucault's definition of sexuality as a simultaneously discursive and material set of institutions. In her estimation, such a description avoids both the essentialist claim that sexuality is natural and the idealist claim that human bodies are in some way not physical.[7] Perhaps more than Foucault himself, however, McNay and other feminist critics emphasize the materiality of the gendered body and the constraints placed by gender norms upon both women and men. In so doing, they maintain a conceptual distinction between sex and gender even while arguing that the two are epistemologically the same: namely, that the only kind of knowledge we can have about biology and gender is mediated by language.

Similarly maintaining and displacing the distinction between sex and gender, Judith Butler explains: "Gender is not to culture as sex is to nature; gender is also the discursive/cultural means by which 'sexed nature' or 'a natural sex' is produced" (*Gender Trouble*, 7). If we accept Butler's definition of the relationship between sex and gender—where one discourse, that of gender roles, encodes and shapes another discourse, that of natural sex—then it follows that without an analysis of gender roles we cannot arrive at a satisfactory understanding of biological sex. This is precisely the blind spot that feminist critics identify in Foucault's work. Consequently, at the same time that they incorporate Foucauldian insights into their own scholarship, feminist critics challenge and compensate for Foucault's own neglect of sexual difference.

If discourses of sex and gender have interactively shaped the modern notion of sexuality as a civic identity, they argue, then examining one without the other cannot yield a satisfactory account of the history of sexuality. McNay is not alone to point out that "If, as Foucault claims, there is no such thing as a 'natural' body and it is, therefore, impossible to posit a pre-given natural sex difference, then he needs to elaborate on how the systematic effect of sexual division is perpetuated by the techniques of gender that are applied to the body" (*Foucault and Feminism*, 33). Armstrong and Riley also accept Foucault's definition of sex as discursive. They fault him, however, for treating the body as if it were gender-neutral, thus failing to explain how men and women relate differently to the institutions of the modern world.

Thus, feminists have found it necessary to revise Foucault's theories in order to make them work for feminism. Foucault defends his "gender-neutral" investigation of sexuality on grounds that the notion of gender is too closely associated with nature to serve as a historical category. Feminists have countered, however, that it is foolish to leave unquestioned the premise that gender identity is natural, for then we have not succeeded in questioning the ontological justifications for a central aspect of modern sexual and civic identity, which was, after all, one of Foucault's primary goals. As Armstrong explains,

> Sexuality is, in other words, the cultural dimension of sex, which, to my way of thinking, includes as its most essential and powerful component the form of representation we take to be nature itself. Thus we can regard gender as one function of sexuality that must have a history. (*Desire and Domestic Fiction*, 11)

In their revision of Foucauldian theory, feminist critics make two closely related arguments, what I would call a theoretical and a pragmatic one. First, they point out that Foucault's strategy of avoiding gender in order to de-naturalize sexuality is logically self-defeating since gender functions as the primary means of naturalizing sex. Thus, the very argument used by Foucault to avoid gender leads feminist critics to explore gender as *the* aspect of sexuality that "includes as its most essential and powerful component the form of representation we take to be nature itself" (11).

In her rereading of Foucault's interpretation of the journal of Herculine Barbin, Butler illustrates that Foucault's neglect of gender leads him to a self-contradictory interpretation of the diary. According to Butler, on the one hand, in most of his work Foucault argues that there is nothing outside of the power relations that produce sexed bodies. On the other hand, and quite inexplicably, he maintains that Herculine's hermaphrodism points to a realm beyond binary sexual identity. Butler states,

> Although he argues in *The History of Sexuality* that sexuality is coextensive with power, he fails to recognize the concrete relations of power that both construct and condemn Herculine's sexuality. Indeed, he appears to romanticize h/er world of pleasures as the "happy limbo of a non-identity" (xiii), a world that exceeds the categories of sex and of identity. The reemergence of a discourse on sexual difference and the categories of sex within Herculine's own autobiographical writings will lead to an alternative reading of Herculine against Foucault's romanticized appropriation and refusal of her text. (*Gender Trouble*, 94)

My reading of Foucault's analysis of Herculine's diary will carry Butler's objection to Foucault's gender-blindness a step further. Indeed, I want to illustrate that what I have called Foucault's first, "theoretical," blind spot concerning gender is related to a second, "pragmatic," blind spot, whereby he fails to examine sufficiently the way gender norms are reproduced in the private and social spheres. I will demonstrate that Herculine's journal can provide what Butler calls "an alternative reading of Herculine against Foucault's romanticized appropriation and refusal of her text" precisely because it belies Foucault's insufficiently critical distinction between masculine and feminine spheres. Foucault argues that, when surrounded by women in convents and Catholic schools, Herculine had relative freedom from gender roles. He suggests that the logic of a "true sex" is imposed upon Herculine by doctors, lawyers, and priests only in the masculine public sphere. In contrast to Foucault's reading, Herculine's own narrative tells us that both feminine and masculine spheres are gendered and impose sexual identity in a similarly restrictive and binary way.

By avoiding gender, Foucault also fails to examine the deployment of sexual discourses in the civic sphere. Consequently, by failing to historicize those feminized spheres along with the masculine public sphere, Foucault misreads not only Herculine's diary but also the modern techniques of sexualization that establish the civic identities he wishes to explore. Feminist critics thus demonstrate that viewing the body as a gender-neutral terrain presents only a masculine version of the history of sexuality and citizenship. Such a history analyzes the regulatory instruments of the public sphere upon public and private life without in turn accounting for the effects of the private sphere upon them.[8]

FEMININE AND MASCULINE SPHERES IN THE DIARY OF HERCULINE BARBIN

Having identified the two major blind spots, theoretical and pragmatic, that feminist critics find in Foucault's scholarship, I propose to account conceptually for their differences. What I want to suggest is that by reintroducing gender into Foucault's genealogy, these critics follow the theoretical model I have described throughout this work. They transform the single dialectical or Hegelian logic of Foucault's analysis of sexuality into a double dialectical logic of sexual difference. The double dialectics reveal that numerous nineteenth-century discourses, including novels, social theories, philosophy, and political tracts, give the sexes both a positive and a negative identity in relation to each other. As we have seen throughout this book, such a reading of gender allows us to understand man as nonwoman, where woman has a positive civic role and man is simply what she is not. Conversely, this model also defines woman as nonman, where man has a positive civic role and woman is simply what man is not. Reading sexuality as a double dialectics of gender enables us to see women not simply as a disempowered or oppressed community, but as something closer to citizen-subjects in their own right.

By way of contrast to Foucault's reading of Herculine's journal, I plan to show that Herculine's self-description observes a double dialectics of gender. Furthermore, I will attempt to prove that only because he ignores the powerful cultural effects of gender upon sex does Foucault propose the hermaphrodite as a model of sexual and civic freedom. Along with Butler, I argue that the hermaphrodite does not step beyond sex or gender into the utopian realm that Foucault calls "a happy limbo of sexual non-identity." My argument will use Foucault's theories against themselves to show that even though biology may not reveal the truth of binary sexual difference, as Foucault demonstrates, the hermaphrodite remains strictly regulated by sex and gender norms in every aspect of her existence.

Only the logic of Herculine's own narrative, which examines the roles played by both sex and gender in nineteenth-century culture, will explain why the hermaphrodite cannot represent a better alternative to modern constructions of sexuality. Androgyny, or hermaphrodism, is neither a harmonious union of two beings in one—the vision of sexual completion that Romantic interpretations have reconstructed from Plato's *Symposium* myth—nor a displacement of gender, as contemporary scholars such as Barthes, Foucault, Derrida, and Cixous would like us to believe. On the one hand, it is obvious from her sad and frustrated narrative that Herculine's sexual confusion does not enable her to feel sexually complete. Quite the contrary, Herculine feels lacking in comparison to sexually differentiated women and men. Because of her sexual "deviance," Herculine feels that she has no legitimate place in a civic order based upon the division of spheres. On the other hand, neither does hermaphrodism enable Herculine to escape gender differentiation, forcing her instead to collide hopelessly with its norms.

Thus, Herculine's narrative demonstrates quite compellingly that the cultural dominance acquired by nineteenth-century discourses of sex and gender cannot be easily eliminated, as those who celebrate androgyny or hermaphrodism indicate. To "unread" Foucault's reading of Herculine's diary, along with the feminist Foucauldians, I insist on the primacy of gender over sex and on the irreducible tension between gender and sexual difference. To do so, however (and here I depart from my predecessors), I will take androgyny as my starting point and show how Herculine's self-description observes a double dialectical process. According to this model, women are defined both positively (as citizen-subjects in charge of social mores) and negatively (as not contributing to the masculine public sphere) with respect to men.

In his analysis of Herculine's journal, Foucault establishes a contrast between the feminine private and social spheres and the masculine public sphere. He accounts for this difference by arguing that "nobody in Alexina's feminine milieu consented to play that difficult game of truth which the doctors later imposed on his indeterminate anatomy" (xiii). In other words, Foucault maintains that nobody in the feminine milieu assigned Herculine a "true sex." Contrasting the relatively "free" sexual experience of Herculine's life as a woman among women with her life as a man among men, Foucault argues that only the doctors and lawyers of the public domain imposed a "true sex" upon Herculine's indeterminate anatomy (xii–xiii). Rather than accept this particular division of spheres, I would like to turn Foucault's dichotomy—between a feminine milieu without sexual injunctions and a masculine milieu with strict sexual codes—into a set of questions.

First, we must consider, is it true that Herculine depicts her life as a student in various women's schools (first a convent, then several Catholic schools) as one of relative sexual freedom and comfort with her sexual indeterminacy? Second, if this is not the case, then what kind of gender logic would lead Foucault to describe the feminine milieu as one untroubled by sexual indeterminacy and the masculine milieu as one intent on establishing natural origins? Were the masculine and feminine spheres worlds apart, as Foucault's analysis would suggest? I will argue that no, this is not what Herculine's account indicates. However much happier she may have been among women, it was not because her indeterminate sex and sexuality were accepted by her peers, as Foucault assumes. Herculine feels happier with the gender role she was socialized to assume—namely, with being (like) a woman, than with being (forcibly) male. It is easier for Herculine to *act like* a woman than to *be* either a woman or a man.

If Foucault misreads Herculine's narrative, then, we are moved to ask, what is the logic of his misreading? I have already suggested that his distinction between a masculine and feminine milieu, and more specifically between Herculine's indeterminate existence as a woman and definitive existence as a man, is overdetermined by a single dialectic of gender. Like a positivist doctor, Foucault establishes the unity of Herculine's identity as a man only by projecting femininity as its contrast, as its indeterminate other side. If in a modern masculine milieu civic identity is determined by the truth of sex, then, according to a single dialectical logic, in a social space populated by women there is no true sex:

> One has the impression, at least if one gives credence to Alexina's story, that everything took place in a world of feelings—enthusiasm, sorrow, warmth, sweetness, bitterness—where the identity of the partners and above all the enigmatic character around whom everything centered, had no importance. (xii–xiii)

Relatedly, Foucault implies, if in a masculine milieu biological sex has the status of a referent that determines identity, in a feminine milieu sex has the nonreferential status of "a world in which grins hung about without out the cat" (xiii). Having defined the modern masculine milieu by means of a single dialectic, Foucault proceeds by the same logic to define male and female citizen-subjects. He explains that "Alexina wrote her memoirs about that life once her new identity had been discovered and established. Her 'true' and 'definite' identity" (xiii). He places Herculine's identity as a woman in opposition to her positively defined identity as a man, claiming "that it is clear that she did not write from the point of view of that sex which had at last been brought to light" (xiii).

Because he assumes that the masculine sex entails a true sexual and civic identity, he also assumes that the feminine sex is defined only negatively, as not being the sex "which had at last been brought to light." In other words, if Herculine has feminine qualities, according to Foucault's reading of gender, that only means that she does not have masculine qualities; if she speaks like or even as a woman, that means that "It is not a man who is speaking, trying to recall his sensations and his life as they were at the time when he was not yet 'himself'" (xiii). In both instances, Foucault regards femininity as the negation of masculinity, not as a separate sexual and civic identity that has positive attributes lacking in a masculine subject or domain.

Foucault's narrative, however, is not consistently androcentric. Like the Hegelian dialectic, it undergoes moments of doubling. At certain moments, Foucault outlines the formation of a feminine citizen-subject by setting Herculine in opposition to a negatively defined masculine subject. Having described femininity as nonmasculinity, Foucault continues to describe Herculine's life as a woman in exactly such terms:

> And what she evokes in her past is the happy limbo of non-identity, which was paradoxically protected by the life of those closed, narrow and intimate societies where one has the strange happiness, which is at the same time obligatory and forbidden, of being acquainted with only one sex. (xiii)

In the first part of the passage, Foucault reinforces his former definition of femininity as "a happy limbo of non-identity," the obverse side of a masculine "true sex." In the second part of this citation, however, the feminine, not the masculine, milieu—namely, "the life of those closed, narrow and intimate societies"—produces the illusion of "being acquainted with only one sex." Curiously, now it is the feminine sphere that is monosexual in relation to an indeterminate and negatively defined masculine sphere. This feminine sphere can be declared monosexual only by acknowledging that it, too, is governed by sex and gender codes that define women as both feminine and female. At this point in his analysis, then, Foucault contradicts his earlier claim that a feminine milieu is less governed by gender codes than a masculine one.

Furthermore, Foucault does not claim that Herculine is like the women around her—otherwise, she would not be a hermaphrodite. Instead he suggests that the similarity among other women emphasizes Herculine's difference from them. The gender logic of the androgyne is shaped by, but cannot conform to, binary gender codes. On the one hand, Herculine cannot be defined as simply nonmale (i.e., as a woman) as Foucault originally sets out to do by means of his dialectical reading of gender: She is nonfemale. On the other hand, as his double dialectical reading of gender illustrates, neither can she be defined as simply nonfemale (i.e., as a man): She is also nonmale.

In moving from a single to a double dialectical understanding of gender, Foucault's narrative reproduces the cultural process that created hermaphrodism as a new category of sexual and civic identity. Though fundamentally unstable, this category can only be established, ironically enough, by stabilizing conventional definitions of masculinity and femininity. In wishing to explain the mechanisms by which we can go beyond gender, Foucault first needs to show us what stable gender categories are. "In this case," he explains, "the intense monosexuality of religious and school life fosters the tender pleasures that sexual non-identity discovers and provokes when it goes astray in the midst of all those bodies that are similar to one another" (xiii–xiv). Herculine's difference can only reinforce the rest of her friends' sameness and, more generally, the similarity of women's bodies and behavior.

Precisely because of his/her gender ambiguity, I now want to argue, the hermaphrodite actually exemplifies the modern sexual subject. It goes without saying that many of us do not have to face Herculine's dilemma of not being able to identify ourselves as being either one sex or the other. Nonetheless, Herculine's narrative underscores something we all do in fact face: the discrepancy between a dialectically defined notion of sexual difference and our inevitable failure to perform gender.

NEITHER FEMININE NOR MASCULINE: THE DOUBLE DIALECTICAL LOGIC OF THE ANDROGYNOUS SUBJECT

Foucault's introduction to Herculine's narrative and Herculine's account of her life collude both in exposing and in obscuring the discourses that mark the hermaphrodite's sex/gender transformations. Both narratives are symmetrically divided into two stages: Herculine's seemingly idyllic existence as a woman in a feminine milieu that tolerates, if not encourages, her "mysterious" sexuality, versus her horrific existence as a man in a masculine milieu that insists upon deciding her "true" sex and eventually leads her/him to commit suicide. Although Herculine describes her experiences among women in highly positive and indeed nostalgic terms, she hardly does so on the basis that femininity is an undefined lack of masculine identity. In fact, sadly enough, the physical perfection she attributes to the women who surround her serves to establish, by way of contrast, her own biological and moral imperfection:

> My childhood and a great part of my youth were passed in the delicious calm of religious houses. Houses that were truly pious, hearts that were pure and true, presided over my upbringing. (3)

Herculine takes great pains to convince herself that, whatever may have been responsible for her deviance, it was not her upbringing. On the contrary, her pious environment established a sharp disjunction between her moral and civic identity (or her gender) and her bodily desires (or her sex).

She laments, "Upon all those young brows I read joy, contentment, and I remained sad, terror-stricken! Something instinctive disclosed itself in me, seeming to forbid me entrance into that sanctuary of virginity" (25–26). A virgin herself, she views herself as corrupted by her own desire for women; educated in a "pious" and "pure" environment, she "instinctively" isolates herself from other women because she regards herself as too impure to be among them.

This internal division, manifested in Herculine's awareness that she does not look or behave like a proper woman, prompts her to define her sexual identity negatively, as nonfeminine in terms of bodily morphology, desires, and moral propensity. Just because she regards herself as lacking in femininity, however, does not imply, as Foucault claims in the first part of his argument, that either Herculine or her companions regard femininity itself as indeterminate. On the contrary, Herculine stands out among the women of the convent only because the codes of femininity are so clearly established there. As she poignantly acknowledges:

> At that age, when all a woman's graces unfold, I had neither that free and easy bearing nor the well-rounded limbs that reveal youth in full bloom. . . . My upper lip and a part of my cheeks were covered by a light down that increased as the days passed. Understandably, this peculiarity often drew to me joking remarks that I tried to avoid by making frequent use of scissors in place of a razor. (26)

In comparing herself to women, then, Herculine thinks of herself negatively, as lacking the (positive) features associated with femininity, including a sensual allure and a well-rounded body. Hardly unaware of the disciplinary mechanisms that produce the feminine body, Herculine and her friends have internalized them well:

> My body was literally covered with [hair], and so, unlike my companions, I carefully avoided exposing my arms, even in the warmest weather. As for my figure, it remained ridiculously thin. That all struck the eye, as I realized every day. I must say, however, that I was generally well liked by my teachers and companions, and I returned their affection fully but in a way that was almost fearful. (27)

In a feminine milieu, Herculine is regarded as nonfeminine, even though no one thinks of her as a man. Insofar as Herculine deviates from the feminine norm, she is viewed, by herself and others, as the exception that helps confirm the femininity of her companions. Her indeterminate sexual identity becomes the subject of curiosity and ridicule, of which Herculine is sadly aware. As she states, "That all struck the eye, as I realized every day." Thus, she constantly surveys her own body, classifying it as unnatural in contrast with the fuller and more properly "feminine" bodies of her friends, who watch her and whom she watches in turn (27). If it has its disadvantages, however, sexual indeterminacy has certain advantages as well, though hardly the freedom Foucault associates with it. Sufficient contrast separates Herculine from her companions, according to the emerging heterosexual framework, to allow for reciprocal distance and desire.

Whereas Herculine's companions observe her with curiosity, Herculine watches her friends with an ever-growing voyeuristic desire that, if we heed psychoanalytic descriptions of the "male gaze," marks her as masculine.[9] Ashamed of her nonfeminine body, Herculine segregates herself from the group activities of her female companions, both to hide her body from their view and to watch and desire their bodies from a nonfeminine position. Ironically, by positioning herself as the subject of the desiring glance (associated with masculinity) while avoiding, as much as possible, the more vulnerable position of an object of others' glances (associated with femininity), Herculine reinforces her lack of femininity. This is, of course, the very quality she wishes, in this gesture, to repudiate when she hides her body from the sight of other women.

The more we find out about Herculine's justifications for her segregation, however, the more we must hesitate to label her as masculine. Though certainly nonfeminine according to a simple binary definition of gender, she is also nonmasculine according to the gender norms of the masculine world. In numerous collective bathing scenes, when "all the girls immediately took off their outer clothing and, wrapping their petticoats around their waists, rushed deep into the beneficial waters" (38), Herculine "was the only one present at this bathing party who was a spectator. What stopped me from taking part in it? A feeling of modesty, which I obeyed almost in spite of myself, compelled me to abstain, as if I were afraid that by joining in this sport I would offend the eyes of those who called me their friend, their sister!" (39). In her voyeuristic activity, Herculine (often involuntarily) assumes a nonfeminine or masculine position by isolating herself from (other?) women, covering her body, and glancing at them with desire. At the same time, she justifies her self-imposed exile in feminine terms, such as modesty (*la pudeur*) and sensitivity to the reactions of her fellow "sisters," both qualities demanded of bourgeois women in the nineteenth century.

In her personal relationships with women, Herculine displays a similarly doubled and contradictory understanding of gender. That Herculine assumes conventionally masculine positions even while trying to approximate the ideal of femininity becomes even more apparent when she cries, in the midst of a passion for her first lover,

"Sara," I cried to her, "from the depths of my soul I love you as I have never loved before. But I don't know what is going on inside of me. I feel that from now on this affection cannot be enough for me! I would have to have your whole life! I sometimes envy the lot of the man who will be your husband." (50)

In assuming the role of the possessive lover, Herculine identifies herself with, but not as, a masculine subject. Her desire to occupy a legitimate masculine subject-position, the civic and sexual identity of a husband, poignantly underscores the impossibility of her doing so. Herculine's ambisexual and at the same time nonsexual position indeed dooms her to "envy the lot of the man who will be [Sara's] husband." Early in the narrative we come to see that she can never be that man. The most she can do is to aspire to womanhood from a position external to but defined in terms of both genders.

Herculine's class position further complicates our reading of her sexual and civic identity. In the context of aristocratic convents, class hierarchies play an important role in her companions' interpretation of Herculine's behavior as feminine. Herculine's affectionate servility toward her aristocratic friends and teachers is interpreted by them as a sign of respect appropriate for a girl of the middle-class toward her social "superiors":

"There," the excellent woman said to me, "you will share the life of girls who are mostly rich and noble. Your companions in study and play will no longer be the nameless children with whom you have lived until now, and no doubt you will soon forget the women who have replaced your absent mother." (6)

In response to this comment about the privilege of being educated and surrounded by aristocratic women, Herculine changes the vocabulary of class into that of sexuality:

I have already said, I believe, that I was particularly fond of the good Sister M., and I could not hear her accuse me like that without being deeply hurt. I had taken her hand, which I clasped in my own, and, unable to explain myself otherwise, for I was violently upset, I brought it to my lips. (6–7)

The mere mention of aristocratic women reminds Herculine of her attraction to them. The nun, however, misinterprets Herculine's response as a properly feminine one, given Herculine's subordinate class position: "This mute protestation reassured her about my feelings, though without making her forget that others were going to have rights to my affection, to my respect" (7). The ambiguous terms *feelings, affection,* and *respect* refer equally well to Herculine's feminine respect for her social superiors as to her masculine desire for the beautiful women who surround her. While Herculine, herself, regards her reaction as a sign of masculinity, the mother superior views it as a sign of feminine deference. What matters most in determining Herculine's sexual identity, at least insofar as her social environment is concerned, is not so much her sexual behavior or physical appearance, as the gender-based standards by which both behavior and body are evaluated.

Hence, upon a closer examination, Herculine's sexual and civic position is not the floating signifier or "the grin without the cat," as Foucault claims, in the sense of being beyond gender conventions. Her passion can perhaps be classified as a floating signifier because it is determined by multiple social codes that interact in a complex and contradictory fashion. As Elizabeth Grosz observes, "[B]odies can be represented or understood not as entities in themselves or simply on a linear continuum with its polar extremes occupied by male and female bodies (with various gradations of 'intersexed' individuals in between) but as a field, a multidimensional continuum in which race (and possibly even class, caste, or religion) form body specifications" (*Volatile Bodies*, 19). Furthermore, in her dynamic and ambivalent subject-positions as a nonfeminine woman who desires women but is not quite a man, Herculine also confuses, rather than clearly violates, the heterosexual imperative.

Herculine understands the nature of her own sexual transgression after making love to Sara for the first time: "Henceforth, Sara belonged to me! . . . She was mine. What, in the natural order of things, ought to have separated us in the world had united us. Try to imagine, if that is possible, what our predicament was for us both!" (51). Herculine understands that she has violated the heterosexual grid defining those who desire men as women and those who desire women as men. She crosses the prescribed boundaries of the "sex/gender system" in three important ways.

First, by virtue of her "inordinate" sexual attraction to women, she violates the heterosexual imperative that dictates that one's own sexual identity is determined by virtue of its polar difference from the object of one's desire. Such forms of identification are the stock-in-trade of psychoanalytic theories that tend to posit, as Judith Butler observes, "that one identifies with one sex and, in so doing desires the other, that desire being the elaboration of that identity, the mode by which it creates its opposite and defines itself in opposition. . . . One either identifies with a sex or desires it, but only those two relations are possible" (*Feminism/Post-Modernism*, 324–340). According to psychoanalysis, desiring and identifying with the same sex, as Herculine ambiguously does, constitutes an aberration. Second, by combining both male and female characteristics, Herculine completely obfuscates any attempt to found gender distinctions upon a natural or biological sexual base. Finally, when she describes her discomfort in a world where women are supposed to be "feminine" and men "masculine," Herculine undermines conventional gender and civic codes.

Herculine's narrative thus challenges three cultural strategies: binary sexual codes, binary gender codes, and the heterosexual imperative. In so doing, it symptomatically discloses the basic conceptual framework of the modern sex/gender system that functions as the basis of modern citizenship.[10] From Herculine's "impossible" gender positions—which, as Foucault urges, we can identify as also our own—sex is already gender. The physical features we associate with "sex" are profoundly affected by, and indeed inseparable from, the social conventions that determine gender. Furthermore, Herculine's journal describes the process by which gender forms are produced in relation to each other. We could say that the hermaphrodite's narrative observes a double dialectics, the first loop of which defines her as a nonfeminine (or masculine) citizen-subject in relation to women. The second loop then reverses this logic to define her as a nonmasculine (or feminine) citizen-subject in relation to men.

If the community of women took femininity as its model of the citizen-subject, the male experts observe a binary logic that adopts masculinity as the standard. Foucault's observation—"[I]t seems that nobody in Alexina's feminine milieu consented to play that difficult game of truth which the doctors later imposed on his indeterminate anatomy, until a discovery that everybody delayed for as long as possible was finally precipitated by two men, a priest and a doctor"—suggests that women are somehow left untouched by the sexual conventions that govern the lives of men (xii). The social standards assumed by the male medical experts who attempt to read Herculine's body, however, are not necessarily more conventional or less tolerant than those assumed by her female companions. They, too, attempt to decode every aspect of Herculine's body sexually, beginning with her facial expressions and features, and moving to the sound of her voice, and to other sexual characteristics (140). The difference between the masculine and feminine evaluations of Herculine's body is not so much their methods of analysis as their points of departure.

The cloistered community of women takes a feminine subject as the norm and defines Herculine's identity as nonfeminine. Homologously, the professional community of men takes a masculine subject as the norm and defines Herculine as nonmasculine. Whereas Herculine's female companions view her as curiously unfeminine but accept her as a woman, the male medical experts think of her as nonmasculine but change her body so that it can be read as male. Their observations painstakingly identify the following sexual attributes:

She has a vulva, labia majora, and a feminine urethra, independent of a sort of imperforate penis, which might be a monstrously developed clitoris. She has a vagina. True, it is very short, very narrow; but after all, what is it if it is not a vagina? These are completely feminine attributes. Yes, but Alexina has never menstruated; the whole outer part of her body is that of a man, and my explorations did not enable me to find a womb. Her tastes, her inclinations, draw her toward women. At night she has voluptuous sensations that are followed by a discharge of sperm; her linen is stained and starched with it. Finally, to sum up the matter, ovoid bodies and spermatic cords are found by touch in a divided scrotum. These are the real proofs of sex. We can now conclude and say: Alexina is a man, hermaphroditic, no doubt, but with an obvious predominance of masculine sexual characteristics. (127–128)

Let us briefly review the gender-based logic that transforms Herculine into Abel. On the one hand, Herculine has a vulva and a urethra. She has never menstruated and bears a nonperforated penis that the experts compare to a monstrously developed clitoris. Thus, they are using the female as the norm. In the next phase of their description, however, the doctors take a heterosexual male as the gender norm and indicate that the fact that she desires women—indeed, the very existence of sexual desire—is male. Finally, the doctors fix on one more piece of evidence: Herculine appears to have a barely formed scrotum. Since the scrotum is, as the doctor phrases it, "the true evidence of sex," then Herculine must really be a Herculin. This analysis leaves us with no choice but to conclude that the sexual characteristics and object choice of men have more to do with determining an individual's sexual and civic identity in the public sphere than those associated with women.

Foucault argues that giving Herculine her supposed "true sex" involves not so much a medical operation as a legal process. From this inference he asks us to conclude that sexuality became the basis of civic identity at this point in history. He appends to Herculine's journal a series of medical articles on Herculine's sexuality in which several doctors, including those who performed her autopsy, describe their findings in juridical rather than medical terms. One doctor who had examined the living hermaphrodite explains:

I do not hesitate to publish it almost in full, as I wish to keep the lesson that it contains from being lost. This is doubly precious, on the one hand from the standpoint of the influence that the malformation of the sexual organs exercises upon the emotional faculties and upon psychological health, and on the other hand from the standpoint of the serious individual and social consequences that may be entailed by an erroneous declaration of the sex of a newborn child. (Auguste Tardieu, *Question médico-légale de l'identité dans les rapports avec les vices de conformation des organes sexuels,* 123)

The doctor argues that physical "malformations" have profound social implications, both for the individual concerned and, more important, for society at large. Such malformations disrupt the gender norms that enable society to divide labor appropriately. If nature fails to distinguish gender, he claims, then it is society's obligation to change nature so that it can provide a foundation for gender. In other words, culture has the power to correct the "errors" of nature.

The doctor who performed Herculine's autopsy argues in a similar vein:

> The autopsy permitted a rectification of the first judgment, which had determined his sexual identity during the greater part of his life, and a confirmation of the exactness of the diagnosis that in the end had assigned him to his true place in society. (131)

Interestingly, this doctor does not go so far as to say that medicine can correct nature. Rather, he interprets Herculine's failure to meet the norms of either masculinity or femininity as a bad reading of the body. As such, the problem posed by the hermaphrodite's sexual and civic identity can be rectified by subsequent evaluations confirming "the diagnosis that in the end had assigned him to his true place in society." Nature, the foundation of positivist analysis, is also a slippery concept that defies legal definition. Consequently, the discourse of nature must be replaced by the discourse of social evaluation, the very discourse that had required nature to establish its credibility.

By reading Herculine's diary against the grain of Foucault, I am moved to ask why both his analysis and Herculine's journal set a feminine community based on difference in opposition to a masculine community based on sameness. In answer to this question, I would have to say that Foucault's distinction between the open-mindedness of Herculine's female companions and the compulsive objectification performed by the male scientific community is symptomatic of a more general modern cultural phenomenon. Herculine's convent sisters and mothers certainly seem to occupy something resembling the traces of an early modern sexual world. This world is based on what Foucault describes as the logic of sexual identification rather than that of biological identity.

Herculine's female friends may consider her body and behavior ridiculous or even disturbing, but they do not attempt to change it, ascribing its differences to class rather than sex. For them, rank evidently matters more than gender in establishing an individual's place in the civic order. Likewise, as Foucault's introduction explains, the male experts create the mechanisms that enable a modern gendered society to function. While granting the fact that Herculine's text produces such a distinction between a lost early modern past and a technocratic modernity, I regard that distinction as the product of modern discourse itself.

In nineteenth-century texts, such an imaginary premodern world is generally represented by children, women, non-Western cultures, the working classes, or country folk: in other words, by those who fall outside of the boundaries of urban bourgeois society. This cultural ambivalence toward an ambiguously gendered past is aptly described by Renato Rosaldo as a form of "imperialist nostalgia":

> Imperialist nostalgia revolves around a paradox: A person kills somebody, and then mourns the victim. . . . When the so-called civilizing process destabilizes forms of life, the agents of change experience transformations of other cultures [or aspects of their own] as if they were personal losses. Nostalgia is a particularly appropriate emotion to invoke in attempting to establish one's innocence and at the same time talk about what one has destroyed.[11]

It is not only Herculine's text that is symptomatic of a nostalgia for the premodern practices that modernity systematically destroys, but also our contemporary texts that, like Foucault's, attempt to distance themselves from these kinds of sentimental gestures. In Herculine's journal, the sense of nostalgia seems particularly overdetermined. Herculine mourns her loss of femininity. This femininity depended on relations with women in a social environment still marked by aristocratic privileges but threatened by bourgeois social mobility, as evidenced by her own interactions with aristocratic girls. Furthermore, such a femininity also allowed her interpersonal relations with women in marked contrast to her impersonal professional ties with men.

As Rosaldo's narrative predicts, Herculine's sense of loss is accompanied by a sense of gain. As her often self-righteous journal entries reveal, in re-creating her free early modern life in the convents, Herculine gains a sense of innocence that appears to position her outside of the alienating and reifying modern social structures and relations she rejects. Yet, as I hope to have illustrated in my discussion of her sexual identifications, Herculine is fully and intricately immersed in the double dialectical social relations that define women as nonmasculine and men as nonfeminine.

Neither she nor her female companions are less socialized—or less modernized—than the male group of experts. Likewise, the ways in which the doctors, scientists, and lawyers evaluate Herculine's body seem no more accurate or free of gender-based preconceptions than the ways her female friends interpret it. Both sets of observations, though seemingly so different, express prevalent beliefs about what constitutes a proper "man" or "woman." In both cases, "man" and "woman" are assumed to be mutually exclusive categories. Although clearly influenced by the same binary sexual and gender codes, the two groups reach different, we might even say opposite, conclusions, if we assume men to be the opposite of women. As we have seen, among female companions Herculine was viewed as a nonfeminine woman; among male experts she was viewed as a nonmasculine man. Her hermaphroditic identity always seemed to incorporate, as well as negate, the gender standards by which her sexuality was assessed.

These different conclusions demonstrate not only the strong social effect of binary gender-based conventions. They also reveal the instability of discourses of "sexual difference," as they are lived out and interpreted according to different registers: including context-based perceptions, partial selections of information considered relevant, and Herculine's changing behavior. According to Jochen Schulte-Sasse, the manner in which we interpret and perform social categories can be compared to a kind of materialist "deconstruction" of dominant conventions:

> Just as the play of signifiers contradicts and undermines any claim of possessing a well-defined, conceptually unequivocal, logocentric discourse, so material experience may contradict and undermine the prevalent ideology of a historical situation. And just as the struggle for interpretive power by imposing metaphysical closures attempts to restrain the play of signifiers, the prevailing ideology limits the means by which individuals may more or less consciously understand their material experiences.[12]

Herculine's interpretations of sexual identity are certainly overdetermined—in the sense of being both motivated and bounded—by interacting and contradictory social discourses and practices. It is the very complexity, contradiction, and multiplicity of her subject-positions that produce both her apparent "freedom" from sex/gender and her unique entanglement in its structures and relations.

Herculine's narrative, in its multiple sexual identifications and confusions, enables us to constantly shift our position between the opposing frames of a double dialectical process of sexual difference that produces a version of citizenship based upon the division of spheres and its androgynous sublation. In so doing, it maps out not so much a strange and deviant sexual identity—the hermaphrodite—as the cultural logic of modern gender roles that we can recognize as our own. Ignoring the effects of gender roles upon Herculine's body, Foucault finds in hermaphrodism a liberating identity that displaces sexual difference. By identifying the double dialectical logic of sex and gender in Herculine's diary, however, one finds that the hermaphrodite is paradoxically defined by the very gender norms her body violates. Only by accepting the conventions of masculinity and femininity entrenched in her culture can Herculine find herself lacking with respect to both.

NOTES

1. Foucault, Introduction to *Herculine Barbin: Being the Recently Discovered Memoirs of a Nineteenth-Century French Hermaphrodite*, trans. Richard McDougall (New York: Pantheon Books, 1980), xi–xii. This is the text from which I will be citing in this chapter.

2. Armstrong, *Desire and Domestic Fiction*.

3. Bartky, "Foucault, Femininity and the Modernisation of Patriarchal Power," in *Feminism and Foucault*.

4. Sawicki, "Identity Politics and Sexual Freedom," in *Feminism and Foucault*.

5. Fraser, *Unruly Practices: Power, Discourse and Gender in Contemporary Social Theory*.

6. McNay, *Foucault and Feminism*.

7. She states, "Following his definition of discourse as an amalgam of the material (power) and non-material (knowledge), Foucault presents in *The History of Sexuality*, a theory of the body and sexuality which is both radically anti-essentialist but, at the same time, does not deny the materiality of the body" (*Foucault and Feminism,* 29). Making a similar argument in *Patterns of Dissonance,* Rosi Braidotti elaborates, "Foucault displaces and expands the notion of materialism, by inscribing it in the corporeality of the subject. In so doing he reveals and denounces a double trap that threatens feminism, like other social political movements: on the one hand a sociologizing reductivism [. . .] that sets the female individual in opposition to the patriarchal system; on the other, the utopian model which makes 'women' an entity (on the) outside, foreign to the dominant system and not contaminated by it" (89). I find it interesting that, by attempting to avoid gender in his analysis of Herculine's sexuality, Foucault falls into the trap of idealizing a feminine social context, much like the feminists he criticizes.

8. Compensating for this simultaneously epistemological and historical blind spot, some feminists have traced women's crucial roles in the development of modern sexual codes, their influence in certain public policies, including education and philanthropy (Riley), and the textual representations of gender in both fiction and conduct books aimed at women, which propose sexual codes and establish the modern sexual identities and familial relations we continue to live out today (Armstrong).

9. See, for example, Mary Ann Doane's analysis of the male and (potentially) the female gaze in *The Desire to Desire: The Woman's Film of the 1940's.*

10. As Judith Butler explains, "The heterosexualization of desire requires and institutes the production of discrete and asymmetrical oppositions between 'feminine' and 'masculine,' where these are understood as expressive attributes of 'male' and 'female.' The cultural matrix through which gender identity has become intelligible requires that certain kinds of 'identities' cannot 'exist'—that is,

those in which gender does not follow from sex and those in which the practices of desire do not 'follow' from either sex or gender. . . . Indeed, precisely because certain kinds of 'gender identities' fail to conform to those norms of cultural intelligibility, they appear only as developmental failures or logical impossibilities from within that domain" (*Gender Trouble,* 17).

    11. Rosaldo, *Culture and Truth, The Remaking of Social Analysis,* 69–70.

    12. Schulte-Sasse, foreword to Peter Bürger, *Theory of the Avant-Garde,* xxvii.

Conclusion:
Androgyny and the Chiasmic
Economy of Sexual Difference

Today, more than ever, we appear to live in an androgynous age. Women vote and hold office while also being maternal. Men are masculine yet sensitive. What seemed to be an impossible combination of masculine and feminine characteristics has become, through historical and dialectical development, simply a new definition of sexual identity. Yet this contemporary identity is neither more nor less androgynous than the one established by writers such as Comte, Balzac, and Sand during the nineteenth century. Today's gender categories bring with them a new series of polarizations: between emotional and reserved; beautiful and handsome; primary and secondary providers; custody and child support. Gender distinctions are not eliminated, just transformed.

To state that the androgynous mixture of former gender traits did not lead to an improvement in women's social status would be disingenuous. To state that this dialectical process will lead to an infinite progress toward human equality would be both meaningless and premature. No one can predict the future of gender; similarly, we cannot yet conceive of what human equality might entail. Nonetheless, examining the development of gender roles as a dialectical process that is intrinsically androgynous enables us to understand better our position as citizens of the modern nation-state. Employed as a descriptive, rather than prescriptive, category, androgyny is neither liberating nor regrettable. It is one of the possible representations of the road that led to where we are today.

Throughout my book, I have argued that the two patterns of gender formation—the single and double dialectics—lead us to acknowledge the fundamental androgyny of the citizen-subject. As I noted in describing

111

Hegel's single dialectic, the implicitly masculine subject depends for its identity upon the partial inclusion as well as the partial exclusion of a feminine subject that is defined as its negative. Judith Butler depicts this process as the formation of a "constitutive exterior": an exterior that is never fully outside because it is internal to the concept whose identity is determined by this exclusion. In Comte's, Balzac's, and Sand's double dialectics of gender, both male and female subjects function as the "constitutive exteriors" of the other sex. That is, the definitions of each sex are formed by means of the negation of the characteristics of the "opposite" sex. If we accept the poststructuralist premise that the concept of "woman" is internal to the concept of "man" and vice versa, then we can say that neither sex can be fully separated from the other sex. Both "men" and "women" are constitutively "androgynous."

This double dialectical approach to an examination of androgyny differs from most previous critical treatments of this subject, which, I would argue, are trapped within a single dialectical model of sexuality. As I have shown, such a model does not adequately account for women's historical role in subject-citizenship during the nineteenth century. Androgyny, a concept derived from the words *andros* (man) and *gune* (woman), generally refers to the combination of masculine and feminine physical and/ or cultural traits in a single being. In both fiction and theory, androgyny tends to be depicted as an exception to the rule. The rule, in turn, entails a structure of sexual difference where the physical and cultural identities of men and women are viewed as different, complementary, or even opposite of one another.

Criticism on the subject of androgyny, most notably provided by the anthology *L'Androgyne: Cahiers de l'hermetisme,*[1] Carolyn Heilbrun's *Toward a Recognition of Androgyny,*[2] and *The Androgyny Papers,*[3] has tended to represent androgyny as a metaphor that symbolizes gender unity. More specifically, androgyny has been portrayed as a harmonious synthesis between male and female characteristics. Viewing androgyny as a synthesis of the sexes generally implied, above all, that the identities of the sexes were a known, if not fixed, aspect of society. Androgyny was not meant to question this gender opposition, but rather to alter its effects by combining male and female qualities. It was assumed that a synthesis of sexual opposites would create a more complete being or society.[4] I would like to argue, however, that the concept of androgyny-as-union proves to be too static a tool, serving more to confirm gender categories than to transform them.

Heilbrun's work in particular treats androgyny as a trope that mixes the two genders utopically. By combining masculine and feminine elements and thus obfuscating gender distinctions, androgyny supposedly levels the hierarchies implicit in most discourses of sexual difference. I would like to demonstrate, however, that gender theories that celebrate androgyny in the way Heilbrun's model does tend to define it as a synthesis of the sexes that operates within a masculine economy. This understanding of androgyny is problematic since, as I have shown, a symbolic economy that begins with a masculine subject and subsequently derives, by negation, a feminine subject cannot be transformed into an economy that values both male and female subjects even in their mixture. Models of androgyny-as-sexual-synthesis are still governed by the dialectical movements of a masculine subject and its feminine Other outlined by Hegel.

In her introduction to *Toward a Recognition of Androgyny*, Heilbrun declares,

> My opinion is easily enough expressed: I believe that our future salvation lies in a movement away from sexual polarization and the prison of gender toward a world in which individual roles and the modes of personal behavior can be freely chosen. The ideal toward which I believe we should move is best described by the term "androgyny." (ix–xi)

Observing that sexual difference is the norm in Western societies, Heilbrun draws a connection between the existing sexual dimorphism and sexual hierarchies. From this correlation, she deduces that a freely chosen mixture of gender characteristics could diminish sexual hierarchies. She thus envisions androgyny as a sexual identity that transgresses, if not transcends, gender positions:

> Androgyny suggests a spirit of reconciliation between the sexes; it suggests, further, a full range of experience open to individuals who may, as women, be aggressive, as men, tender; it suggests a spectrum upon which human beings choose their places without regard to propriety or custom. (xi)

Although Heilbrun's conclusion that transgressing gender norms can be liberating is plausible, her argument faces conceptual as well as the obvious pragmatic difficulties. She reasons that if, when sexual characteristics are rigidly assigned, men are privileged over women, it follows that if gender distinctions were confused, men and women would acquire equivalent value. There are, however, at least two problems with this conclusion. First, it is difficult to change gender norms without questioning the sexual (or biological) identities of man and woman that tend to buttress such conventions.[5] In other words, the terms *man* and *woman* necessarily carry a lot of baggage about "masculinity" and "femininity" that justifies gender conventions. Consequently, before androgyny can be offered as a solution to gender hierarchies, the relations between "nature" and "culture," or in this case between the naturalized concepts of "men" and "women" and their attributes of "masculinity" and "femininity," have to be critiqued.

The second problem faced by Heilbrun's argument is related to the first. Since she takes the qualities of "masculinity" and "femininity" as the elements that can be intermixed to create "androgyny" without examining the formation of sexual dimorphism itself, she does not offer a clear description of androgyny, which represents, after all, the product of the mixture of sexual identities. Without interrogating sex, Heilbrun cannot effectively critique gender. Once we examine Heilbrun's definition of androgyny more closely, we see that both its problems arise from its single dialectical logic that continues, in spite of itself, to privilege a masculine subject.

By defining androgyny as "a spirit of reconciliation between the sexes," Heilbrun leaves intact the assumption that the sexes exist in an oppositional relationship. By itself, this assumption need not entail a gender hierarchy. In arguing, however, that the masculine subject is culturally dominant—which is the thrust of her (or any) feminist critique—she implies that definitions of the subject begin with masculinity. Putting together these two assumptions, we can deduce that the feminine subject represents the negation (or opposite) of an original and culturally dominant masculine subject. Androgyny, then, constitutes the synthesis between that masculine subject and his feminine negation (or opposite). This definition leaves the feminine subject without a separate identity. Heilbrun has described the process of gender formation that arrives at her version of liberating androgyny as a single dialectic, much as Hegel has done. And like the Hegelian model of gender, Heilbrun's formulation of cultural androgyny also leaves no space for feminine difference. If we begin with gender categories produced by a masculine subject that undergoes repeated negations and incorporations, it is difficult to see how we can use androgyny to accomplish a feminist goal, namely, to create a nonsexist society that respects both women and men.

Perceiving the difficulties inherent in the concept of androgyny, feminist and cultural criticism never really picked up this figure to shift the dissymmetry of gender difference. Such criticism rejected androgyny in favor of two opposing strategies: (1) ignoring gender because it is a category that is too easily regarded as natural as opposed to historical (the Foucauldian approach), or (2) emphasizing women's identity as distinct from men's (Irigaray's differentialist approach). My book has combined aspects of both approaches. Transforming Irigaray's metaphor of sexual reciprocity into a dialectical method of reading gender, I have shown that, contrary to Foucault's fears, androgyny is not an intrinsically essentialist and ahistorical trope. In fact, androgyny overcomes the impasse between essentialism and anti-essentialism and between historicism and antihistoricism. I will first explain how androgyny can serve as a tool for understanding the cultural history of gender. Furthermore, since cultural history can still be essentialist—if it assumes the existence of foundational sexual traits—I will then proceed to argue that the concept of androgyny is also unessentialist.

Looking at subject-citizenship in terms of two kinds of androgyny called attention to the historical transition from relational definitions of gender that are asymmetrical (and necessarily privilege one gender at the expense of the other) to those that are symmetrical (and tend to accommodate both male and female subjects on equivalent terms). We have called a single dialectical pattern androgynous insofar as the category of women is intrinsic to all definitions of men. According to this form of androgyny, women do not have a cultural identity of their own since there is never any point at which men come to represent the external limits of the category women. Only in a system in which each gender negates the other can both become fully acknowledged as citizen-subjects.

Second, only by differentiating these two kinds of androgynies can we trace the cultural shift from an alliance-based patriarchal model of the family predicated upon a division between the feminine private sphere and the masculine public sphere (elaborated by Hegel's single dialectics of gender) to a nuclear model of the family that contains the latent possibility for including both women and men in definitions of subject-citizenship (elaborated by Sand's, Comte's, and Balzac's double dialectics of gender). This cultural transition from one model of gender and family relations to another is neither historically linear nor conceptually clear-cut. My reading of various nineteenth-century texts has identified the moments where Comte's and Balzac's double dialectical models of gender continue to assume the masculinity of the citizen-subject, thus undermining the logic contained by the chiasmus.

Third, once we have understood gender as constitutively androgynous, we have also come to realize that the division of spheres is never complete. The category "male" can never be fully separated from the category "female." Proceeding on this understanding, we may be able to come up with better reasons for women's exclusion from modern citizenship. More specifically, this book has identified women's more complex and, to use Joan Scott's term, "paradoxical" positioning in relation to the public arena. Let us say, we enter this world with androgynous, and hence impure and even self-contradictory, sexual identities. Then it would be only through a repeated enactment of norms and practices that we become socialized as men and women, believing that a narrow set of biological differences should shape almost every aspect of our lives, from dress, to bodily gestures, to professions. It goes without saying that the distinction between men and women is not a natural given, but a complex task that requires constant cultural work.

This brings us to the fourth intellectual benefit of looking at gender as androgynous. Such a perspective can provide feminist theory with additional grounds of questioning the natural or essentialist justifications for sexual hierarchies. Discourses of sexual difference must be critically examined because sexual difference has been effectively represented as the natural origin or cause of gender-based conventions, such as the division of spheres and the historical exclusion of women from political self-representation. Rather than assuming that because sexual dimorphism and hierarchies exist and, to our knowledge, have existed in every society, sex and gender relations have to have a natural or universal basis; looking at gender as androgynous has illustrated that societies continue to generate such complex systems of laws, customs, and institutions to prescribe sexual difference because it has insufficient basis in nature.

The position that the manner in which gender norms come into being has little or no basis in "nature" undermines both essentialist and constructionist explanations of gender relations. We reverse the cause-and-effect explanation for gender norms when we observe that sexual difference arises from a complex set of sociopolitical motivations that are only tenuously related to human biology. The objective is not so much to offer alternative answers to these questions than the ones provided by either feminist or nonfeminist texts as to explore the contradictions and cultural and political effects of these kinds of questions. Such an interrogative approach to gender enables us to displace the foundations of discourses of sexual difference, which usually rely upon ontological or biological paradigms of gender in order to justify either sexual hierarchies or, in feminist discourses, their displacement.

Second, and perhaps more important, the trope of androgyny enables us to explain why the debates regarding gender have been so important in Western history. Gender has functioned as the foundation of modern citizen-subjects, but this foundation, I have argued, is not foundational after all. To counter the tendency to accept sexual difference as the natural cause of gender-based thinking, I have shown that sexual difference is the absent origin[6] of gender laws. Sexual difference is thus everywhere assumed, sought, and implemented, but nowhere ontologically found with epistemological (rather than simply ideological) certainty. Consequently, gender identity is neither completely founded in the reproductive differences between men and women nor completely attributable to arbitrary cultural factors. Gender is thus truly the result of an absent origin: a field of probabilities where the reproductive differences and interdependency between men and women may have influenced gender norms, but where gender norms—and particularly their hierarchical nature—cannot be explained, but only, as we have seen in nineteenth-century texts, retroactively justified, in terms of the biological differences between men and women. This epistemological openness concerning the causes of discourses of sexual difference has functioned as a point of departure for my study of their cultural and political effects upon formulations of subject-citizenship in nineteenth-century France.

Androgyny, the chiasmus, and the double dialectics all narrate the same historical and conceptual transformation in models of citizenship. The moment that gave rise to a basically Hegelian view of women as the negation of man also saw the development of a positive representation of femininity that anticipated the arguments produced by contemporary theorists such as Luce Irigaray, Denise Riley, and Joan Scott. In this double dialectical representation of gender inherited from diverse nineteenth-century texts—including not only the works of Comte, Balzac, and Sand, but also the diary of Herculine Barbin—woman is portrayed as playing a unique civic role in culture. Rather than rendering her simply non-masculine, such a representation gave woman a positive cultural identity that she never before possessed.

NOTES

1. *L'Androgyne, cahiers de l'hermétisme,* Antoine Faivre and Fréderick Tristan, eds. The latest important work that addresses at length the problematic of androgyny is Kari Weil's *Androgyny and the Denial of Difference.* My book is similar to hers in that it employs the concept of androgyny to critique identity-based understandings of sexual difference. In this respect, both my work and Weil's can be situated in the tradition of poststructuralist scholarship that demonstrates that masculinity and femininity do not constitute separate identities. Weil uses both Barthean and Derridean theories of androgyny to show the instability of gender. By way of contrast, my work performs a dialectical reading to explain the formation of sexual difference and of modern citizenship.

2. Carolyn Heilbrun's *Toward a Recognition of Androgyny* traces the use of the trope of androgyny in Western literature beginning with Homer, to Shakespeare, and ending with the modernist representations of Virginia Woolf and Thomas Mann. Heilbrun argues that the intermixture of gender offers a good solution to current gender divisions and their inevitable accompanying hierarchies. For Heilbrun, a recognition of androgyny entails a recognition of the role of femininity in Western civilization, a recognition that would render our appreciation of Western cultures not only less androcentric, but also more complete.

3. In 1973 a group of feminist scholars organized a special forum on androgyny at the MLA convention and subsequently published the papers in *The Androgyny Papers* (found in *Women's Studies,* Cynthia Secor, ed.).

4. I am referring here, once again, to some of the most influential androgyny myths or discussions of androgyny, ranging from Plato's *Symposium* to Virginia Woolf's Platonic vision of androgyny in *A Room of One's Own*, to the contemporary discussions of androgyny mentioned previously. For an analysis of these representations of androgyny that my study will not duplicate, see Kari Weil's *Androgyny and the Denial of Difference*.

5. This argument is persuasively made by Judith Butler in *Gender Trouble: Feminism and the Subversion of Identity* and *Bodies That Matter: On the Discursive Limits of "Sex."*

6. In *Only Paradoxes to Offer*, Scott explains the "absent origin" of gender norms in terms of a circular cultural logic: "As a result, law substituted for truth as a guide in human action. But this substitution was not acknowledged as such; instead whatever law passed was said to be based upon nature or truth . . . By a kind of circular logic a presumed essence of men and women became the justification for laws and policies when, in fact, this 'essence' (historically and contextually variable) was only the effect of those laws and policies" (ix–x).

Bibliography

Accampo, Elinor A. "Gender, Social Policy, and the Third Republic." In *Gender and the Politics of Social Reform in France, 1870–1914,* Elinor A. Accampo, Rachel G. Fuchs, and Mary Lynn Stewart, eds. Baltimore: Johns Hopkins University Press, 1995.

Anderson, Benedict. *Imagined Communities: Reflections on the Origin and Spread of Nationalism.* London: Verso, 1983.

Armand-Duc, Nicole. "The Law's Contradictions." In *A History of Women in the West: Emerging Feminism to World War,* Geneviève Fraisse and Michelle Perrot, eds. Cambridge: Harvard University Press, 1993.

Armstrong, Nancy. *Desire and Domestic Fiction.* Oxford: Oxford University Press, 1987.

Aron, Raymon. *Main Currents in Sociological Thought: Montesquieu, Comte, Marx, Tocqueville.* New York: Basic Books, 1965.

Ashford, Douglas E. *The Emergence of the Welfare States.* Oxford: Blackwell, 1986.

Balzac, Honoré de. *La Cousine Bette.* Paris: Gallimard, 1972.

Bartky, Sandra. "Foucault, Femininity and the Modernisation of Patriarchal Power." In *Feminism and Foucault: Reflections on Resistance,* I. Diamond and L. Quinby, eds. Boston: Northeastern University Press, 1988.

Beiser, Frederick C. "Hegel's Historicism." In *The Cambridge Companion to Hegel,* Frederick C. Beiser, ed. Cambridge: Cambridge University Press, 1993.

Benhabib, Seyla. *Situating the Self: Gender Community and Postmodernism in Contemporary Ethics.* New York: Routledge, 1992.

Berlin, Isaiah. *Four Essays on Liberty.* London: Oxford University Press, 1969.

Béteille, Arlette. "Où finit *Indiana*? Problématique d'un dénouement." *Recherches nouvelles: Groupe de recherches sur George Sand.* C.R.I.N. 6–7 (1983): 62–73.

Bethke, Jean. *Public Man, Private Woman: Women in Social and Political Thought.* Princeton: Princeton University Press, 1981.

Bhaskar, Roy. *Reclaiming Reality: A Critical Introduction to Contemporary Philosophy.* London: Verso, 1989.

Bloch, Ernst. *The Utopian Function of Art and Literature: Selected Essays,* Jack Zipes and Frank Mecklenburg, trs. Cambridge: MIT University Press, 1988.

Bloss, Thierry, et al. *La Femme dans la société française.* Paris: Presses Universitaires de France, 1994.

Blum, Carol. *Rousseau and the Republic of Virtue: The Language of Politics in the French Revolution.* Ithaca, N.Y.: Cornell University Press, 1986.

Butler, Judith. *Gender Trouble: Feminism and the Subversion of Identity.* New York: Routledge, 1990.

———. *Bodies That Matter: On the Discursive Limits of "Sex."* New York: Routledge, 1993.

Carrard, Philippe. *Poetics of New History.* Baltimore: Johns Hopkins University Press, 1992.

Chonez, Claudine. "George Sand et le féminisme." *Europe* 587 (March 1978): 75–79.

Comte, Auguste. *A General View of Positivism,* J. H. Bridges, tr. New York: Robert Speller and Sons, 1957.

Coser, Lewis A. *Masters of Sociological Thought: Ideas in Historical and Social Context.* New York: Harcourt Brace Jovanovich, 1971.

Doane, Mary Ann. *The Desire to Desire: The Woman's Film of the 1940's.* Bloomington: Indiana University Press, 1987.

Donzelot, Jacques. "The Promotion of the Social." *Economy and Society* 17 (August 1988): 404.

———. *L'Invention du social.* Paris: Fayard, 1984.

Faivre, Antoine, and Fréderick Tristan, eds. *L'Androgyne, cahiers de l'hermétisme.* Paris: Albin Michel, 1986.

Fauré, Christine. *Democracy without Women: Feminism and the Rise of Liberal Individualism in France,* Claudia Gorbman and John Berks, trs. Bloomington: Indiana University Press, 1991.

Findlay, J. N. Foreword to G. W. F. Hegel, *Phenomenology of Spirit,* A. V. Miller, tr. Oxford: Oxford University Press, 1977.

Foucault, Michel. Introduction to *Herculine Barbin: Being the Recently Discovered Memoirs of a Nineteenth-Century French Hermaphrodite,* Richard McDougall, tr. New York: Pantheon Books, 1980.

———. *The History of Sexuality: An Introduction,* Robert Hurley, tr. New York: Vintage Books, 1990.

Fraisse, Geneviève. *La Raison des femmes.* Paris: Plon, 1992.

———. *Muse de la raison: La Démocratie exclusive et la différence des sexes.* Aix-en-Provence: Alinéa, 1989.

Fraser, Nancy. *Unruly Practices: Power, Discourse and Gender in Contemporary Social Theory.* Minneapolis: University of Minnesota Press, 1989.

Furet, François. *Revolutionary France 1770–1880,* Antonia Nevill, tr. Oxford: Blackwell, 1993.

Gaillard, Françoise. "La Science: Modèle ou vérité, Réflexions sur l'avant-propos à *La Comédie humaine.*" In *Balzac: L'Invention du roman.* Paris: Pierre Belfond, 1982.

Giddens, Anthony. *The Giddens Reader*. Philip Cassell, ed. Stanford, Calif.: Stanford University Press, 1993.

Hayek, F. A. *The Counter-Revolution of Science: Studies on the Abuse of Reason*. New York: Free Press of Glencoe, 1964.

Hegel, G. W. F. *Phenomenology of Spirit*, A. V. Miller, tr. Oxford: Oxford University Press, 1977.

———. *Philosophy of Right*, T. M. Knox, tr. Oxford: Oxford University Press, 1967.

Heilbrun, Carolyn. *Toward a Recognition of Androgyny*. New York: W. W. Norton, 1973.

Hunt, Lynn. *The Family Romance of the French Revolution*. Berkeley: University of California Press, 1992.

Irigaray, Luce. *J'aime à toi*. Paris: Grasset, 1992.

———. *Speculum: De l'autre femme*. Paris: Les Editions de Minuit, 1974.

Jameson, Fredric. *The Political Unconscious: Narrative as a Socially Symbolic Act*. Ithaca: Cornell University Press, 1981.

Kojève, Alexandre. *Introduction à la lecture de Hegel*. Paris: Gallimard, 1947.

Landes, Joan. *Women and the Public Sphere in the Age of the French Revolution*. Ithaca: Cornell University Press, 1988.

Lloyd, Genevieve. *The Man of Reason: "Male" and "Female" in Western Philosophy*. Minneapolis: University of Minnesota Press, 1984.

Lukacs, Georg. *The Historical Novel*, Hannah and Stanley Mitchell, trs. Lincoln: University of Nebraska Press, 1983.

———. *The Theory of the Novel: A Historico-Philosophical Essay on the Forms of Great Epic Literature*, Anna Bostock, tr. Cambridge: MIT University Press, 1992.

———. *Toward the Ontology of Being*, David Fernbach, tr. London: Merlin Press, 1978.

Marcuse, Herbert. *Reason and Revolution: Hegel and the Rise of Social Theory*. Atlantic Highlands, N.J.: Humanities Paperbacks, 1957.

Marshall, T. H. *Class, Status and Citizenship*. New York: Anchor Books, 1965.

McClintock, Anne. *Imperial Leather: Race, Gender and Sexuality in the Colonial Context*. New York: Routledge, 1995.

McGuire, James R. "The Feminine Conspiracy in Balzac's *La Cousine Bette*." *Nineteenth-Century French Studies* (1981): 295–296.

McNay, Lois. *Foucault and Feminism*. Boston: Northeastern University Press, 1992.

Mill, John Stuart. *Auguste Comte and Positivism*. Ann Arbor: University of Michigan Press, 1965.

Miller, Christopher L. *Blank Darkness: Africanist Discourse in French*. Chicago: University of Chicago Press, 1985.

Mozet, Nicole. "*La Cousine Bette*: Roman du pouvoir féminin?" In *Balzac et les parents pauvres*, Françoise van Rossum-Guyon and Michiel van Brederode, eds. Paris: Société d'Edition d'Enseignement Supérieur, 1981, 33–45.

Oxford Encyclopedic English Dictionary. Oxford: Oxford University Press, 1991.

Pateman, Carole. *The Disorder of Women: Democracy, Feminism and Political Theory*. Stanford: Stanford University Press, 1989.

———. *The Sexual Contract*. Stanford, Calif.: Stanford University Press, 1988.

Petrey, Sandy. "George and Georgina Sand: Realist Gender in *Indiana*." In *Sexu-*

ality and Textuality, Michael Worton and Judith Still, eds. Manchester: Manchester University Press, 1994.

Plato. *Symposium,* Walter Hamilton, tr. New York: Penguin, 1951.

Preminger, Alex, ed. *The Princeton Handbook of Poetic Terms.* Princeton: Princeton University Press, 1986.

Proudhon, P. J. *Du principe de l'art et de sa destination sociale.* Paris: Garnier, 1865.

———. *Les Femmelins: Les Grandes figures romantiques.* Paris: A l'écart, 1989.

Rabine, Leslie. "George Sand and the Myth of Femininity." *Women and Literature* 4 (1976): 2–17.

Rescher, Nicolas. *Ethical Idealism: An Inquiry into the Nature and the Function of Ideals.* Berkeley: University of California Press, 1987.

Riley, Denise. *Am I That Name? Feminism and the Category of "Women" in History.* Minneapolis: University of Minnesota Press, 1988.

Rockmore, Tom. *Hegel's Circular Epistemology.* Bloomington: Indiana University Press, 1986.

———. *On Hegel's Epistemology and Contemporary Philosophy.* Atlantic Highlands, N.J.: Humanities Press, 1996.

Rosaldo, Renato. *Culture and Truth, The Remaking of Social Analysis.* Boston: Beacon Press, 1989.

Rose, Gillian. *Dialectic of Nihilism in Post-Structuralism and Law.* London: Blackwell, 1984.

Rousseau, Jean-Jacques. *Emile, ou de l'éducation.* Paris: Garnier-Flammarion, 1966.

Salomon, Pierre. *George Sand.* Paris: Hatier-Borcier, 1953.

Sand, George. *Histoire de ma vie.* In *George Sand, Oeuvres autobiographiques.* Georges Lubin, ed. Paris: Gallimard, 1971.

———. *Indiana.* Paris: Gallimard, 1984.

Sawicki, Jana. "Identity Politics and Sexual Freedom." In *Feminism and Foucault: Reflections on Resistance,* I. Diamond and L. Quinby, eds. Boston: Northeastern University Press, 1988.

Schor, Naomi. *Bad Objects: Essays Popular and Unpopular.* Durham, N.C.: Duke University Press, 1995.

———. *George Sand and Idealism.* New York: Columbia University Press, 1993.

———. *Reading in Detail: Aesthetics and the Feminine.* New York: Routledge, 1989.

Schulte-Sasse, Jochen. Foreword to Peter Bürger, *Theory of the Avant-Garde.* Minneapolis: University of Minnesota Press, 1992.

Schwartz, Joel. *The Sexual Politics of Jean-Jacques Rousseau.* Chicago: University of Chicago Press, 1984.

Scott, Joan W. *Only Paradoxes to Offer.* Cambridge: Harvard University Press, 1996.

Secor, Cynthia, ed. *Women's Studies,* special issue, *The Androgyny Papers* 2 (1974).

Sewell, William H., Jr. "Le Citoyen/la citoyenne: Activity, Passivity, and the Revolutionary Concept of Citizenship." In *The Political Culture of the French Revolution,* vol. 2, Colin Lucas, ed. New York: Pergamon, 1988.

Standley, Arline Reilein. *Auguste Comte.* Boston: Twayne Publishers, 1981.

Suvin, Darko. *Metamorphoses of Science Fiction: On the Poetics and History of a Literary Genre.* New Haven: Yale University Press, 1979.

Taine, Hippolyte. *Derniers essais de critique et d'histoire.* Paris: Hachette, 1894.

———. *Philosophie de l'art.* Paris: Ressources, 1980.

Thomas, Edith. *George Sand*. Paris: Editions Universitaires, 1959.

Weil, Kari. *Androgyny and the Denial of Difference*. Charlottesville: University of Virginia Press, 1992.

Wood, Allen W. "Hegel's Ethics." In *The Cambridge Companion to Hegel*, Frederick C. Beiser, ed. Cambridge: Cambridge University Press, 1993.

Woolf, Virginia. *A Room of One's Own*. New York: Harcourt, Brace, Jovanovich, 1957.

Zizek, Slavoj. *The Sublime Object of Ideology*. London: Verso, 1989.

Index

About the Author

Claudia Moscovici is assistant professor of humanities at Boston University. Her research interests include Enlightenment and nineteenth-century French literature and philosophy, representations of gender, and theories of democratic citizenship. Her publications, including *From Sex Objects to Sexual Subjects* (Routledge, 1996), focus on models of citizenship in modern French literature and culture.